Of Two Minds

The Dead Sea Scrolls &
Christian Origins Library
1

Of Two Minds

Ecstasy and Inspired
Interpretation in the
New Testament World

by

John R. Levison

With a Foreword
by
James H. Charlesworth

BIBAL Press

North Richland Hills, Texas

BS
480
.L47
1999

BIBAL Press
An imprint of D. & F. Scott Publishing, Inc.
P.O. Box 821653
N. Richland Hills, TX 76182
1–888–788–2280
info @dfscott.com
www.dfscott.com

Printed in the United States of America
03 02 01 00 99   5 4 3 2 1

Library of Congress Cataloging-in-Publication Data
Levison, John R.
 Of two minds : ecstasy and inspired interpretation in the new
testament world / by John R. Levison ; with a foreword by James H.
Charlesworth.
    p. cm. — (The Dead Sea scrolls & Christian origins library ; 2)
Includes bibliographical references.
 ISBN 0-941037-74-6
 1. Bible. O.T.—Inspiration. 2. Inspiration—Religious
aspects—Judaism. 3. Ecstasy (Judaism) 4. Bible. O.T.—Criticism,
interpretation, etc., Jewish. 5. Judaism—History—Post-exilic period,
586 B.C.-210 A.D. 6. Philo, of Alexandria—Contributions in concept of
Biblical inspiration. 7. Greek literature, Hellenistic—Influence. I.
Title. II. Series.
 BS480 .L47 1999
 296.3'115—dc21
                                                      99-050560

Images copyright © 1999 by www.arttoday.com

To
Louis H. Feldman

consummate scholar,
generous friend

Contents

Foreword

Can Divinities Play Human Vocal Chords Like Harps?

Professor John R. Levison has written a fascinating and insightful book. It focuses on early Greek, Roman, and Jewish attempts to explain the ability of some humans to possess superhuman, or divine, knowledge and insight. From Plato's *Symposium* we hear that divine beings communicate "divine things to humans." In the *De divinatione* Cicero's brother, Quintus, claims that some have received "a heaven-inspired excitement and exaltation of soul." In Plutarch's *De defectu oraculorum* Lamprias argues that the soul, especially when freed from the body in dreams or near death, can see and speak with the powers of another world.

These reflections by Greeks who lived in the Hellenistic and Roman Periods help us comprehend how some Jews, like Philo and Josephus, can resolve complexities and inconsistencies in biblical Hebrew. While the author of Numbers 22–24 does not tell us how Balaam could produce an oracle, Philo and Josephus both relate how *an angel* possessed Balaam and moved his vocal chords so that he prophesied what he did not know. Similarly, the author of the *Liber Antiquitatum Biblicarum* creates episodes in which the minor character Kenaz explodes with superhuman skills and prophesies, by means of the Holy Spirit, a pellucid view of the future. Kenaz has this vision, as Lamprias had suggested, just before his death.

Inspiration—especially scriptural inspiration—is a central issue in this monograph. Jews and Christians throughout the world claim that the Bible is inspired. But this claim is often ambiguous, and a wide range of meanings is attributed to it. How does God inspire a person? And how do we distinguish between inspired words and personal speculation in the Bible—two categories found, for example, in Paul's writings.

What did Philo mean when he claimed that Moses was wise because he was guided by a spirit? And what did Plutarch intend by claiming that Socrates' wisdom derived from a "demon" who was his guide? What is the meaning of Simmias' claim, in Plutarch's *De genio Socratis* 588 D-E, that Socrates' understanding was so free from bodily passions that the demon could make "voiceless contact with his intelligence"?

Levison rightly points out that attempts to comprehend biblical inspiration involve reflections upon the power of the human intellect, the purity of the soul, and the possession of wisdom. These were discussed respectively by Plutarch in *De genio Socratis*, by Cicero in *De divinatione*, and by Diogenes Laertius in *Lives of the Philosophers*, and by Philo in *Plant*. In Early Judaism, Wisdom was often the term used to comprehend intellect and inspiration. For some Jews, Wisdom was personified, either finding no home on earth (*1 Enoch*) or residing in inspired Torah (Ben Sira, see *2 Baruch*).

What is the meaning of the claim that the inspired person immediately loses knowledge of what was said and how it was spoken? Why is this claim espoused by Greeks, Romans, Jews, and Christians for centuries in antiquity? And what is memory? How can Ezra, according to the author of *4 Ezra*, dictate from memory alone twenty-four Hebrew books lost during the burning of Jerusalem in 70 CE and 70 additional inspired works?

Does inspiration entail forgetfulness? Or, is this pervasive claim merely a clever attempt to underscore the claim that the speaker is not the source of the thought, but another—and someone divine?

FOREWORD

Some biblical authors imply that inspiration comes through dreams. This is a hotly debated issue in Greek and Roman thought, as Levison illustrates. It is also a point of contention among some Jews. For example, Ben Sira flatly denies that dreams can be a source of wisdom and understanding, while the authors of Daniel, *1 Enoch*, and *2 Enoch*, among others, clearly affirm it.

In surveying Plato, Cicero, and Plutarch, and scanning Ben Sira, Philo, the author of the *Liber Antiquitatem Biblicarum*, and Josephus, and in delving into such universal probes into the power of the human mind, we may comprehend the impact of Greek and Roman thought upon early Jewish theology. In the process, we grasp a little more clearly the vibrant world in which Judaism was being transformed and Christianity formed.

Much more than biblical inspiration is involved in the reflections gathered in this stunning monograph. Profound questions bubble up on almost every page. How much truth is in Plato's claim that inspired poets are ignorant of the meaning of their poems? (*Apology* 22C and *Meno* 99C)? Why do loved ones we have known claim to see something unusual and make startling claims just prior to their deaths? How has God communicated to the inspired men and women immortalized in the Bible? How does God speak to us today? What is meant by non-verbal communication—or the language of silence?

The search for some understanding of inspiration is pervasive in the history of humanity. How could Muhammad, a brilliant but illiterate Arab, compose such a masterpiece as the Koran? What is meant by the claim that he dictated what he heard from a divine voice? And, how are his claims different from those associated with Socrates, Ezekiel, Jesus, and Isaac Newton? What did Mozart mean when he claimed he was not composing but copying what he heard? Why did Einstein claim that his major creative thought did not derive from science or mathematics but from inspiration?

FOREWORD

Some ancients claimed that only the "insane" could become inspired. What is the deeper meaning here? What are the borders between genius and insanity?

This present monograph is admirably focused. It needs to be continued and expanded. For example, the world of Plotinus needs to be included, and his claim that the soul can ascend and obtain pure knowledge needs reflection and discussion. Also, there is the whole world of Gnosticism, which is no longer to be discarded as nonsense or heresy. What is the meaning of the gnostic claim that knowledge entails returning to a former world in which knowledge was pure and the soul once again whole?

The ancient scholar Cleombrotus suggested that a formerly inspired person could no longer speak inspired words because he or she was simply like a musical instrument that now lies unused—like a harp resting in a corner of a room. This reflection may help us understand inspiration only partly and collapses, as do all analogical reflections. With Lamprias, we need to know how the inspired person is like an instrument, how and why does it begin to speak, and who causes the sound to appear.

J. H. Charlesworth
Editor, Princeton Dead Sea Scrolls Project and
Alexander von Humboldt Fellow
Institut für antikes Judentum und hellenistische Religionsgeschichte
Tübingen

Preface

Late in the first century CE, a Jewish writer concluded his lengthy, emotional response to the fall of Jerusalem by recounting, "...when I had finished all the words of this letter and had written it carefully until the end, I folded it, sealed it cautiously, and bound it to the neck of the eagle. And I let it go and sent it away" (2 Bar 87:1). The finality of folding, sealing, and sending away a manuscript, even if it be sent undramatically by post rather than eagle's neck, is never simple. It represents the irretrievability and irreversibility of ink and paper, binding and glue. It represents as well an opportunity for pause and reminiscence, for recalling the communities in which an author has lived while poring over texts ancient and modern. It is primarily upon the people of those communities that I intend to dwell very briefly before binding this slender volume to the neck of the eagle, so to speak, and sending it off.

I have known, first of all, the pleasure of perusing the reflections of ancient philosophers and civic leaders, such as Philo Judaeus, Seneca, Cicero, and Plutarch, of ancient historians, such as Flavius Josephus and the Jewish author of the *Liber Antiquitatum Biblicarum*, and of scribes, such as Jesus Ben Sira. I hope in this book to clarify two particular dimensions of these ancient figures: their grasp of the inspiration of the mind, on one hand, and on the other, the surrender of the mind under the spell of divine inspiration.

Alongside the camaraderie of these ancient figures, I have been privileged to experience as well the critique and encouragement of contemporary communities of scholars. The catalyst for my first foray into this area of research occurred in 1992 at the Yeshiva University in New York City, under the auspices of a Summer Seminar for College Teachers funded by the National

Endowment for the Humanities. There I worked among eleven other scholars under the capable direction of Louis H. Feldman, professor of classics at Yeshiva University. His considerable mastery of ancient sources, his celebration of critique, his unparalleled bibliographical reach—all enhanced by a wry wit—catalyzed my own interest in this research.

A year later, I was afforded the opportunity to enter another community—the Institut für Antikes Judentum und hellenistische Religionsgeschichte of the Eberhard-Karls-Universität Tübingen, under the direction of Professor Hermann Lichtenberger. During that sojourn, I was wrested from teaching responsibilities, favored with a quiet study, and granted unlimited library privileges in the Theologicum. None of this was entirely my doing. Professor Larry Hurtado had written on my behalf to Professor Martin Hengel, who took it upon himself to sponsor me, sight unseen, for an exceptionally generous stipend from the Alexander von Humboldt Foundation, and then who, along with Marianne, his gracious wife, extended hospitality to me and to my family on innumerable and memorable occasions.

While I have labored to present my research afresh in this book, it contains nonetheless ideas and analyses which appear in a more technical format in earlier publications. I cite them here primarily to credit those journals and publishers, as well as to suggest further reading for those whose interest is piqued by this volume: "The Debut of the Divine Spirit in Josephus' Antiquities," *Harvard Theological Review* 87 (1994) 123-38; "The Prophetic Spirit as an Angel According to Philo," *Harvard Theological Review* 88 (1995) 189-207; "Prophetic Inspiration in Pseudo-Philo's *Liber Antiquitatum Biblicarum*," *Jewish Quarterly Review* 85 (1995) 297-329; "The Angelic Spirit in Early Judaism," in *1995 SBL Seminar Papers* (Scholars Press) 464-93; "Inspiration and the Divine Spirit in the Writings of Philo Judaeus," *Journal for the*

PREFACE

Study of Judaism 26 (1995) 271-323; "Josephus' Interpretation of the Divine Spirit," *Journal of Jewish Studies* 47 (1996) 234-55; and *The Spirit in First Century Judaism*, AGAJU 29 (Leiden: E. J. Brill, 1997).

I am especially grateful to James H. Charlesworth, of Princeton Theological Seminary, who, as editor of this series, offered me the opportunity to render this research accessible to a wider audience than those publications are intended to reach. The important task of seeing this book to completion, moreover, fell to William Scott, of BIBAL Press. I thank both of them for procuring photographs, for editing the volume thoroughly, and for the unseen labor expended to bring this volume to fruition.

Though she would not welcome it, I cannot in good conscience neglect to express my thanks to Priscilla, my wife. Although her responsibilities are ample as my colleague at Duke University Divinity School and as the mother of our children, Chloe and Jeremy, Priscilla has remained doggedly interested in this research and its implications. I consider myself a uniquely fortunate man to be the husband and colleague of such a woman as Priscilla, who possesses a winsome personality, an acute scholarly edge, and an uncanny knack for brewing delicious coffee.

J. R. Levison
The Divinity School
Duke University
Durham, North Carolina

Abbreviations

Amat.	Plutarch, *Amatorius*
Ant.	Josephus, *Antiquitates Judaicae*
2 Bar	2 (Syriac Apocalypse of) Baruch
BCE	Before Common Era (=BC)
Bell.	Josephus, *Bellum Judaicum*
CA	Josephus, *Contra Apionem*
CE	Common Era (=AD)
Cher.	Philo, *De cherubim*
Def. Orac.	Plutarch, *De defectu oraculorum*
Div.	Cicero, *De divinatione*
Ebr.	Philo, *De ebrietate*
1 En	1 Enoch
Fug.	Philo, *De fuga et inventione*
Gaius	Philo, *De legatione ad Gaium*
Gen. Soc.	Plutarch, *De genio Socratis*
Gig.	Philo, *De gigantibus*
Her.	Philo, *Quis rerum divinarum heres*
Immut.	Philo, *Quod Deus immutabilis sit*
Jos.	Philo, *De Iosepho*
LAB	*Liber Antiquitatum Biblicarum*
Leg. All.	Philo, *Legum allegoriae*
LXX	Septuagint
Mig.	Philo, *De migratione Abrahami*
MT	Masoretic Text
Mut.	Philo, *De mutatione nominum*
Nat. Deor.	Cicero, *De natura deorum*
Opif.	Philo, *De opificio mundi*
Plant.	Philo, *De plantatione*
Post. Cain	Philo, *De posteritate Caini*
Ps(s)Sol	Psalm(s) of Solomon
Ps-Justin	Pseudo Justin
Pyth. Orac.	Plutarch, *De Pythiae oraculis*
1QH	Qumran Hymns
11QMelch	11 Q Melchizedek
1QpHab	Habakkuk Commentary
1QS	The Rule of the Community
Som.	Philo, *De somniis*
Spec. Leg.	Philo, *De specialibus legibus*
TAbr, TAsh, TBen	Testament of Abraham, Asher, Benjamin
TDan, TGad, TLevi	Testament of Dan, Gad, Levi
Virt.	Philo, *De virtutibus*
Vit. Mos.	Philo, *De vita Mosis*

Introduction

The title of this slender volume, *Of Two Minds*, suggests the breadth of impact that was accorded to the spirit in a variety of early Jewish literary texts. The "first mind" represents the mind lost to ecstasy, the mind overcome by the spirit, the mind unconscious in the spirit's presence. This is the topic of the second chapter in this book—on inspired ecstasy—where we shall observe how creatively and carefully Jewish authors from Rome, Alexandria, and Palestine imported into their Bibles a conception of ecstasy that was far more at home at Delphi in Greece than in ancient Israel. The "second mind" represents the mind engaged in the process of interpretation, the mind heightened by the spirit to interpret ancient texts, the mind whose acuity is strengthened by the presence of the spirit. This is the topic of the third chapter of this book—on inspired interpretation—in which we shall observe how several early Jewish authors, from the author of Nehemiah in the fourth century BCE to the author of 4 Ezra at the end of the first century CE, recognized the divine spirit as the source of an inspired interpretation of Scripture. The choice of the title, *Of Two Minds*, is, therefore, an apt indication of the span of the spirit's impact—from the ecstasy of inspiration to the inspiration of interpretation.

The Variety of Jewish Authors and Texts

The brief compass of this volume does not lend itself to a detailed description of the authors and literary texts that will be studied in the following two chapters. Nonetheless, a brief introduction to each should prove beneficial in the navigation of literature that spans several centuries, arises from diverse geographical regions, and attempts to meet various goals.

Philo Judaeus' stature among the Jewish Alexandrian community resulted in his heading a delegation to visit the Roman emperor Gaius Caligula in Rome in 39/40 CE following an anti-Jewish pogrom in Alexandria under the prefect Flaccus in 38 CE. From this and other events of less certain date, it appears that this Jewish statesman was probably born between 20 and 10 BCE and died approximately 50 CE. Although he was compelled to participate in public life, such as this delegation, Philo preferred the role of philosopher and biblical interpreter. Therefore, he dedicated himself to a prolific production of treatises in three areas:

- Explanation of the Mosaic laws, including the story of creation, history, and legislation;

- Commentaries on the Bible, most of them intended to provide allegorical interpretations of Genesis;

- Other more thematic treatises on such philosophical topics as the nature of providence and historical topics such as the embassy Philo led to Gaius.

Philo's treatises and commentaries indicate that he had a thorough Roman education, for they contain frequent allusions to ancient Greek literature, such as the dialogues of Plato.[1] For example, he understood the plural form, "Let us make," in Gen 1:26 to mean that God employed subordinates to create a composite human being, which can tend either to virtue or to vice, so as not to impute responsibility for evil to God. This conception of creation by subordinates stems from Plato's *Timaeus* 41–42 (*Opif.* 72–75). The interpretations of the spirit that we shall encounter in this book serve unequivocally to confirm this impression of the cosmopolitan character of Philo's life and literature.[2]

While Philo and his contemporaries were occupied with the anti-Jewish pogrom in Alexandria, **Flavius Josephus** was born in 37 CE to a pre-eminent priestly family in Jerusalem (*Vita* 1–2). Following brief forays at the age of sixteen into the various Jewish schools—Pharisees, Sadducees, and Essenes— Josephus spent three years with the desert hermit, Banus, then returned to opt for Pharisaism (*Vita* 10–12). Like Philo, though perhaps less reluctantly, Josephus was thrust into the political arena when, at the age of twenty-six, he participated in an embassy to Rome, where he moved in Rome's privileged circles (*Vita* 16). Josephus subsequently participated in the Jewish War against Rome (66–73/4 CE), first as a Jewish general, then, after defecting to Rome, as a counselor to the Romans against the Jews. Following the war, Josephus was taken to Rome, granted citizenship, and lodged in the Flavian household, with the emperor Titus as his benefactor. In Rome, Josephus wrote a self-exonerating account of the Jewish revolt of 66–73/4 CE and the events leading up to it in the *Jewish War* (*Bellum Judaicum*). After the death of Titus, under the benefaction of Epaphroditus, Josephus composed three works: the *Antiquities*, a voluminous revision of Jewish history from creation to the first century CE; his autobiography (*Vita*), intended principally to explain his defection to the Romans during the Jewish War; and *Contra Apionem*, in which he refuted many of the libels that circulated amongst the Greco-Roman opponents of the Jews. Throughout these writings, Josephus showed a keen acquaintance with non-Jewish literature, from Greek stories of creation to Egyptian versions of the exodus to the commentaries of recent emperors such as Titus.[3]

The manuscripts and early editions of *Liber Antiquitatum Biblicarum* (LAB) were incorrectly ascribed to Philo Judaeus; the unknown author of this work is, therefore, referred to as Pseudo-Philo. This narrative retelling of the Bible, from creation to the death of Saul, was probably composed in Hebrew in Palestine during the late first or early second century CE. A significant theme of the work consists of a polemic against idols. For example,

the minor judge, Jair, about whom little is recorded in Judg
10:3–5, becomes a ruler who built an altar to Baal and
decreed, "Everyone who will not sacrifice to Baal will die"
(38:1). Despite this intransigent rejection of foreign idols,
Pseudo-Philo did not "lead a cloistered life. His work is
filled with evidence of the influence on him of the
non-Jewish world about him."[4] The lament of Jephthah's
daughter (Judg 11:34–40) in LAB, for example, exhibits
close similarities to a Greek tradition of laments for girls
who died young, such as Iphigenia in Euripides' *Iphigenia
at Aulis*, Cassandra in Euripides' *Daughters of Troy*, and
Antigone in Sophocles' *Antigone*.[5] *Liber Antiquitatum
Biblicarum*, therefore, combines a zeal for the God, cove-
nants, and commands of Israel with a resilience toward
Greco-Roman culture.[6]

The biblical book of **Nehemiah** contains one verse
(9:20) that is of extraordinary import for this study. The
books of Ezra and Nehemiah, which were originally considered a single literary work, recount events that took place in
Palestine, beginning with the dedication of the Temple in
515 BCE and extending probably into the late 400s BCE.
Therefore, the book of Nehemiah must have been written in
Palestine sometime later, probably between 400 and 300
BCE. Neh 9:20 is set in a lengthy prayer of confession that
begins with creation and concludes with the exile.

Ben Sira was a scribe who led an academy or scribal
school in the city of Jerusalem. The book of Sirach, or
Ecclesiasticus, is a compilation of his teaching that was
probably completed by 175 BCE, for Ben Sira made no reference to the subsequent treacherous anti-Jewish actions of
Antiochus IV Epiphanes (175–64 BCE). His grandson
translated this book from its original Hebrew to Greek during the decades after 132 BCE. Although this compilation
has no clear principal of organization, it falls into three
major portions: chapters 1–24; chapters 25–43, which
follows a long poem about wisdom (24); and 44–50, in
which Ben Sira praises Israel's ancestors. Although Ben
Sira traveled a great deal and was no doubt concerned
about the destabilizing impact of Greco-Roman culture on

Jews, he himself was receptive to that culture, such as when he adopted the Stoic principal of divine cosmic unity in his theology by writing, "We could say more . . . let the final word be: 'He [God] is the all'" (43:27). This dual commitment to universal truth and Jewish faith is nowhere more evident than in the hymn of wisdom, in which Ben Sira described universal wisdom, located her dwelling in Jerusalem, and then identified her with Torah (24:1–23). The reference to scribal inspiration that concerns us in this book, Sir 39:6–11, is part of a lengthy description of the scribal task which probably contains several autobiographical elements (38:24–39:11) and thus may inform us both about scribal self-identity and Ben Sira's self-perception.[7]

In 1947, a Bedouin in the regions just west of the Dead Sea discovered the first of many scrolls in caves near the Dead Sea. These documents are now commonly called the **Dead Sea Scrolls**. These caves contained scrolls and many fragments of biblical books (e.g., Isaiah), apocryphal texts (e.g., Sirach), and pseudepigraphical texts (e.g., *Jubilees*). Among these scrolls as well were those that probably express the identity of the Qumran community itself: commentaries on biblical material (e.g., on Habakkuk); commentaries on texts clustered around specific themes or figures (e.g., Melchizedek); texts employed in the definition and regulation of the Community (e.g., *Damascus Document*; *Rule of the Community* [*Manual of Discipline*]; *Temple Scroll*); eschatological texts (*War Scroll*); and texts concerning worship (e.g., calendrical texts; *Thanksgiving Hymns*). From these scrolls, it appears that the Community began its life at Qumran sometime during the second century BCE and continued until 68 CE, during the Jewish War with Rome. The *Thanksgiving Hymns*, which comprised one of the seven original scrolls discovered in Qumran Cave I, contain some of the references relevant to the topic of inspired interpretation, for these poems, which are modeled on the biblical psalms and begin with a word of praise or thanks, reveal a keen interest in the attainment of knowledge.[8]

Written within a generation after the destruction of Jerusalem in 70 CE, possibly in Palestine, *4 Ezra* consists of a dialogue between the figure of Ezra (the post-exilic scribe) and Uriel, the angelic representative of God. Seven visions comprise this book, all of them related to the theological problem raised by the destruction of Jerusalem at the hands of the Romans. The first three are dialogues between Ezra and the angel in which Ezra refuses to accept Uriel's answers about human sin and divine management of the world; the next three are symbolic visions which lead Ezra ultimately to give "great glory and praise to the Most High because of his wonders" (13:57); the seventh vision recounts in detail Ezra's inspired ability to restore the twenty-four biblical books and seventy others that were destroyed during the destruction of Jerusalem. In this final vision, we encounter the detailed and profound conviction that the activity of the Holy Spirit persists in the wake of national and cultic annihilation, for "the spring of understanding, the fountain of wisdom, and the stream of knowledge" (14:47) emerge from the books that Ezra dictates to his scribal associates.[9]

The Impact of the Greco-Roman Environment

Although these two modes of inspiration by the divine spirit—the ecstasy of the seer and the inspiration of the scholar—are the focal points of this study, this book comprises also a fascinating exposé of the encounter between Judaism and its Greco-Roman environment. This book will document how Greco-Roman conceptions of inspiration had a deep impact upon some of these Jewish authors, particularly the author of *Liber Antiquitatum Biblicarum*, Philo, and Josephus. Although this impact was neither uniform nor uncritical, the Jewish encounter with Greco-Roman culture could not leave Judaism unchanged.[10] In order to trace this impact accurately, I have derived the mass of evidence from three treatises of two Greco-Roman authors, Cicero and Plutarch, which were written between the years, 100 BCE and 100 CE.

Cicero, who was born on January 3, 106 BCE and died on December 7, 43 BCE, wrote the treatise, *De divinatione*, to explore the nature of divination, which he had passed over in an even more comprehensive treatment of religion, *De natura deorum* (see *Div.* 1.8–9; 2.3). Quintus, Cicero's brother and an advocate for the Stoic position, defines divination as "the foreseeing and foretelling of events considered as happening by chance" (1.9). He distinguishes between two forms of divination: artificial, which employs methods of divination such as augury, astrology, and the examination of entrails; and natural divination, which is produced by mental excitement and dreams (1.12). The validity of both, contends Quintus, demonstrates two related propositions: "if there is divination, there are gods . . . if there are gods, there is divination" (1.10, 82–83). In particular, the gods communicate with humankind, and divination is the means by which humans interpret the gods' signs.

Of particular import for our study is *De divinatione* 1.37–71 and 1.110–21, in which Quintus discusses natural divination. He is concerned to dispute the inference that a few false dreams invalidate the entire enterprise. This concern leads Quintus to argue, on a negative note, that untrustworthy dreams come to ill-prepared people and that unskilled interpreters misconstrue the meaning of dreams and oracles (1.60 and 1.116–21). On a positive note, Quintus contends that people must be properly prepared to receive dreams and inspiration. The details of this latter point are of extraordinary significance for the present study: the souls of such people have developed their innate kinship with the cosmos and receive dreams and oracles when they are freed from the body and stimulated by some external, divine impulse (1.60–67; 1.114–15; 1.129–30).

Plutarch was born in approximately 46 CE. Throughout his life, he maintained particularly close ties with the oracular shrine at Delphi and held a priesthood from 95 CE until his death sometime in the 120s CE. In light of this intimate relationship to Delphi, it is not surprising that he devoted several of his dialogues to topics related to Delphi. In *De E apud Delphos*, he interpreted the word EI at the shrine's entrance. In *De Pythiae oraculis*, he sought to explain why the priestess no longer responded to queries in verse. And in *De defectu oraculorum*, he addressed the problem of diminished oracular activity at Delphi, "or rather the total disappearance of all but one or two; but we should deliberate the reason why they have become so utterly weak" (411E). Of the four responses to this question which Plutarch proffered, two are particularly significant for understanding the conceptions of ecstasy in chapter two of this book, in which we shall study the interpretation of Balaam offered by Philo and Josephus, as well as the contours of Kenaz's vision in *Liber Antiquitatum Biblicarum*.

In *Def. Orac.* 414F-418D (see also 431A-B; 435A; 436F-437A), one of the figures in the dialogue, Cleombrotus, introduces into the discussion a race of demons or demigods who share both "human emotions and godlike power" and mediate between the gods and humankind. Cleombrotus attributes the decrease in oracular activity to their departure from Delphi; when these good demons leave a shrine, the oracles lose their powers, but when they return later, "the oracles, like musical instruments, become articulate" once again.

Another participant in the discussion, Lamprias, presents the Stoic explanation of inspiration. He begins with the innate capacity of the soul to discern the future when it separates from the body through the impetus of an external influence, the divine *pneuma*. In Stoic terms, this "spirit" is a vapor that issues from air or water (*Def. Orac.* 431E-434C). For a variety of physiological reasons, these lakes and springs and vapors, which contain the impetus of inspiration, dry up and disappear. Lamprias attributes the obsolescence of oracles at Delphi to just such a cause, to the intermittent activity of the famous vapor at Delphi. This point of view, like those in *De divinatione*, will lend remarkable insight into the nature of inspired ecstasy.

Plutarch's interest in matters of religion was not limited solely to Delphi. Plutarch's preoccupation with religion characterized him, even early in life, as the discussion of Socrates' inspiration in one of his earlier works, *De genio*

Socratis, reveals. In this dialogue, *De genio Socratis*, Plutarch presented a detailed discussion of the nature of Socrates' inspiration: "but what, my dear sir, do we call Socrates' sign [*to daimonion*]?" One of the participants in this discussion, Simmias, conjectures that the *daimonion* is "the unuttered words of a demon, making voiceless contact with his intelligence," which is free from bodily distractions and passions. Simmias cautions that "the messages of demons . . . find an echo in those only whose character is untroubled and soul unruffled . . ." Simmias recognizes that this interpretation of inspiration differs from popular belief, according to which people receive inspiration when asleep (588C-589F). As evidence for this interpretation, Simmias reluctantly summarizes the myth of Timarchus of Chaeroneia, in which the guiding demon identifies those stars which float above the abyss as the demons of understanding people whose souls are not entirely submerged in passions. Of these demons, some float erratically because they are tethered to unruly souls. Other demons, however, are ordered because they are tethered to responsive, obedient souls from which come the race of diviners and inspired people (589F-592F). These discussions are extremely important for ascertaining Philo's perception of the divine spirit's impact upon Moses and upon Philo himself.

These three treatises of Cicero and Plutarch will, therefore, be indispensable for interpreting several of the Jewish literary works that will be taken up in the ensuing pages. Cicero and Plutarch have bequeathed an unparalleled repository of conceptions about inspiration during the Greco-Roman era.

Now that we have set out the cast of characters that occupy the stage of our study, we may begin. The drama of how conceptions of inspiration unfolded, from the ecstasy of the seer to the interpretations of inspired scholars, promises to hold our attention rapt because each literary text carries its own weight of creativity, its own venturesome quality, just as much as each is tied to the immense and varied literary tradition that emerged during the Greco-Roman era in the diversity of literary texts represented by this small—and significant, I hope—volume.

2 The Inspired Ecstasy of the Seer

Hints of the experience of ecstasy are strewn throughout the literary landscape of early Jewish authors. The Bible, however, affords only rare and ambiguous glimpses of those experiences of ecstasy. In the eighth century BCE, Hosea criticized Israel for saying, "The prophet is a fool, the man of the spirit is mad!" (9:7), and Micah contrasted his own being filled with power and "the spirit of the LORD" with false prophets' inability to obtain visions and revelations, the disgrace of the seers, and the shame of the diviners (3:5–8). Exilic prophets may also have laid claim to experiences of ecstasy. Deutero-Isaiah (Isaiah 40–55) commanded a hearing because "the LORD God has sent me and his spirit" (48:16), while Ezekiel claimed that "the spirit lifted me up" (3:12, 14) in a vision and that "the spirit of the LORD fell upon me" (11:5). These biblical descriptions are muted, however, shedding minimal light on the particular experiences of these prophets.

Other biblical texts which contain more detailed descriptions of the psychological agitation of prophets and seers hint as well at the possibility of ecstatic experiences: Jeremiah's heart beat wildly (4:19); he had an incurable wound (15:18); Isaiah experienced what seemed like birth pangs, accompanied by a reeling mind and trembling (21:3); Habakkuk trembled within, and his lips quivered while his steps trembled (3:16). Some of the most detailed descriptions of this sort of experience are to be found in the biblical book of Daniel, which was probably written during the period of the Maccabean Rebellion (ca. 166–161 BCE), that is, after Ben Sira had compiled his book of wisdom. In the book of Daniel, Daniel's spirit was troubled and terrified (7:15); he entered a trance, prostrate on the ground (8:17–18), lay down sick (8:27), lacked strength (10:8–9), and was speechless and prostrate (10:15–17). The characteristic feature of Daniel's experiences is that these states *follow* a vision rather than, with the onset of ecstasy, precipitating a vision.

Two autobiographical prophetic reflections may signal the onset of ecstasy. In Jeremiah 20:9, the prophet cried out, "If I say, 'I will not mention him [God], or speak any more in his name,' then within me there is something like a burning fire shut up in my bones; I am weary with holding it in, and I cannot." Jeremiah was not, however, talking about an ecstatic experience but about a compulsion to preach words of judgment (20:10). The second text, Ezek 3:14, depicts Ezekiel's transport to Babylon: "The spirit lifted me up and bore me away; I went in bitterness in the heat of my spirit, the hand of the LORD being strong upon me." In this prophetic reflection, heat may suggest the experience of ecstasy—though that signal is by no means obvious.

Other clues to the presence of ecstasy in the Jewish scriptures may appear in the story of King Saul, in which both a good spirit and an evil spirit in 1 Samuel 10–19 were capable of bringing about a state marked by a loss of mental control. Saul, under the influence of the good spirit, prophesied with a band of prophets who utilized musical instruments—harp, tambourine, flute, and lyre—perhaps to induce some form of ecstasy (1 Sam 10:5–6). Some sort of destructive trance may be implied as well in descriptions of the effects which the evil spirit had on Saul, who tried to pin David to the wall with his spear when the evil spirit was with him (18:10; 19:9). In Saul's last encounter with Samuel and the band of prophets, Saul seems to have entered some sort of trance: Saul stripped, prophesied, and lay naked (19:23–24).

What these biblical texts suggest is that, although ecstasy may have been part of the prophetic experience, biblical descriptions are muted, and the presence of ecstasy must be spun out of intimations and suggestive phrases. Only in the case of Saul does that experience appear to constitute a form of trance or ecstasy—but here there is apparently no speech, no vision, no dream to communicate subsequently to a band of hearers.[1] The following explorations of early Jewish descriptions of ecstasy will reveal both *how much more central* a role ecstasy can play in later retellings of the Jewish Bible and how much that emphasis upon ecstasy is due to *the impact of the Greco-Roman environment* upon Judaism.

According to Numbers 22–24, which contains the biblical story of Balaam and the ass, Balak, king of Moab, sent emissaries to Balaam, a noted seer, to obtain from him an oracle that would defeat Israel, Balak's enemy (22:7–21). Balaam set off on his ass, not without equivocation, and was confronted on the way by an angel. Ironically, the ass perceived the angelic presence, but Balaam did not. Balaam, therefore, continued until the angel blocked the way, causing the ass to lie down. In anger Balaam struck the ass, which addressed him with human language (22:22–30). Then "the LORD opened the eyes of Balaam, and he saw the angel of the LORD standing in the road . . ." (22:31). The angel subsequently permitted Balaam to continue on his journey to meet the king of Midian but commanded him to speak only what the angel would tell him to speak (22:35). Balaam delivered four oracular speeches, all of them extolling Israel, including the prediction that a star would come out of Jacob and crush the Midianites, with whom Balak was allied (24:17).

Perplexing ambiguities beset this narrative. Though a travelogue of sorts, the journey is jagged, begun with the approval of God (22:20) but interrupted immediately by God's angel, who confronted Balaam disapprovingly in a walled path between two vineyards. This encounter introduces an element of ambiguity into the narrative, for now the process by which Balaam was capable of delivering oracles becomes confused. Originally God had commanded, "Do only what I tell you to do" (22:20); subsequently the angel commanded, "Speak only what I tell you to speak" (22:35). The angel did not reappear, however, to spark Balaam's oracles; instead, God "put a word into his mouth"

(23:16), and, prior to the third oracle, the spirit of God "came upon him" (24:2).

Equally troubling is the focus of this tale—central to Israel's self-consciousness as a blessed nation—on a diviner (Josh 13:22) who hailed from the Euphrates (Num 22:5) and journeyed to Moab to deliver oracles at the request of a foreign king who ruled Israel's enemies. Further, the responsibility for sparing the Midianite women who seduced Israel, led them to idolatry, and consequently brought about a plague which killed twenty-four thousand (Num 25:1–9) is attributed to Balaam in Num 31:16. How could it be that the angel of God would instruct Balaam (22:35), or that the spirit of God would come upon him (24:2), or that God would "put a word into his mouth" (23:16)—an experience promised the true prophet in Deut 18:18 and denied diviners and soothsayers (18:9–14)? This jarring dissonance, which so violates the principle of prophecy espoused in Deuteronomy 18, led the author of Deuteronomy to another explanation of Balaam's blessing. Balaam cursed rather than blessed Israel, but God thwarted Balaam's efforts by refusing to listen to the curse and by transforming it into a blessing: "the LORD your God turned the curse into a blessing for you, because the LORD your God loved you" (Deut 23:6). The author of Deuteronomy makes no attempt to salvage Balaam; Balaam cursed, God blessed.

Other explanations of Balaam's experience arose during the post-biblical era. The problems of the source of Balaam's oracles and the incorrigible character of this seer led early Jewish biblical interpreters in a direction that very nearly burst the old wineskin of the biblical text with robust new wines that matured during the Greco-Roman era.[2] The products are indeed intoxicating, celebrations of creativity. Two of these Jewish authors, Philo and Josephus, modify Numbers 22–24 by means of different methods. Philo moves in sequence, adapting and altering details as they arise in the biblical text. Josephus takes his more typical tack, placing a speech into Balaam's mouth which announces Josephus' point of view. Despite these differing methods of modifying the biblical text, the interpretations of Josephus and Philo concur remarkably about both the source of Balaam's oracles and the state in which he found himself when he delivered his oracular blessings of Israel. Both authors identify the angel of Num 22:35 with the spirit of Num 24:2 (or LXX 23:7)[3] and characterize Balaam as having entered a state of ecstasy.

The Angel and the Spirit

Philo eliminates the ambiguity of the multiple sources of Balaam's oracles—God, the angel, the spirit—which is inherent in the biblical text, by drawing a close relationship between the prediction of the angel and its fulfillment by the spirit. The prediction of the angel in *Vit. Mos.* 1.274 and its accomplishment by the prophetic spirit in *Vit. Mos.* 1.277 describe the same event, the former in anticipation and the latter in retrospect. In an expanded version of Num 22:35, the angel predicts: ". . . I shall prompt the needful words without your mind's consent, and direct your organs of speech as justice and convenience require. I shall guide the reins of speech, and, though you understand it not, employ your tongue for each prophetic utterance" (*Vit. Mos.* 1.274). This prediction is fulfilled when Balaam "advanced outside, and straightway became possessed, and there fell upon him the truly prophetic spirit which banished utterly from his soul his art of wizardry" (*Vit. Mos.* 1.277). Philo creates this direct correspondence between the prediction of the *angel* and its fulfillment by the divine *spirit* by eliminating the intervening references to God in Num 22:38 and 23:5, according to which God placed a word in Balaam's mouth. In Philo's version, the angel who had promised to prompt Balaam's words, direct his vocal organs, guide the reins of speech, and employ his tongue actually accomplished this when it reappeared, designated appropriately in this new context as the prophetic spirit.

Josephus arrives at a similar identification of the angel and spirit of Numbers 22–24, though by different means. He carefully draws a parallel between the initial approach of the *divine angel* and the ass's perception of the *divine spirit*:

> But on the road an angel of God confronted him in a narrow place, enclosed by stone walls on either side, and the ass whereon Balaam rode, conscious of the divine spirit approaching her, turning aside thrust Balaam against one of these fences, insensible to the blows with which the seer belabored her . . . (*Ant.* 4.108).

In this summary, Josephus shows no reluctance to use the expressions, "angel of God" and "divine spirit," inter-changeably.[4]

In Philo's *De vita Mosis* and Josephus' *Antiquities*, there-fore, the source of inspiration is not, as in the Bible, God, whose dominant presence eclipses the impact of the angel and spirit. Instead, Philo and Josephus through independ-ent means transform the character of the divine spirit. After identifying the angel which appears to the ass with "the divine spirit" (*Ant.* 4.108), Josephus attributes Balaam's oracles to "the divine spirit" (4.118) and "the spirit of God" (4.119). In Philo's *De vita Mosis*, the angel appoints itself the source of Balaam's oracles (1.274), and Balaam is then overcome, in explicit fulfillment of the angel's prediction, by this "prophetic spirit" (1.277).

The Experience of Ecstasy

Another question which Philo and Josephus address con-cerns the *process* by which Balaam's oracles were produced. About this process, Numbers 22–24 offers precious little detail. The angel commanded Balaam to utter only what the angel would say (22:35). The remaining descriptions are brief and formulaic. The first and second oracles occurred because "the LORD put a word in Balaam's/his mouth" (23:5, 16). Similarly, Balaam's repeated retort to Balak, that he spoke only what God put into his mouth (23:12) or what he heard from God (23:26; 24:13), pro-vides little clarification because it too consists of formulaic language drawn from the description of the true prophet in Deut 18:18: "I shall put my words in the mouth of the

Above: Socrates. According to Plutarch, a "demon" (*daimonion*) spoke silently to him, imparting insight to his advanced soul.

Right: Cassandra. She was distinguished in Greco-Roman writings by her ability to predict the future under a violent form of inspiration.

Delphi
An imaginative illustration of the inspired female prophet
in a trance.

Delphi
The abode of the inspired female prophet.

Above: Cicero. This Roman sage wrote about the pros and cons of believing in inspiration.

Right: Plutarch. During the first century, this intellectual pondered the source of Socrates' inspiration and wisdom.

Balaam
His ass perceived the angel's presence before he did,
according to Numbers 22–24.
(Painting by J. James Tissot.)

Balaam

He is shown here blessing, rather than cursing, Israel because—according to Philo and Josephus—an angel controlled his voice.
(Painting by H. Flandrin.)

Othniel

The author of the *Liber Antiquitatum Biblicarum* elevates Kenaz, Othniel's father, and explains how he was inspired. (In the Bible, Othniel is inspired.)

Saul
The first king of Israel was often depicted
as inspired and possessed.
(Nineteenth-century illustration by Gustave Dore.)

prophet, who shall speak everything that I command." The attribution of Balaam's third oracle to the spirit, "Then the spirit of God came upon him" (Num 24:2; and the second oracle, according to LXX 23:7), is described in equally formulaic language. Expressions similar to "the spirit of God came upon him" occur, for example, in Judg 3:10; 11:29; 1 Sam 16:16; 19:9, 20, and 23. The precise process according to which Balaam was inspired, then, is unclear.

Philo and Josephus concur with respect to the resolution they discover to dispel this lack of clarity. According to Philo, as we observed, the angel was displeased with Balaam and said:

> Pursue your journey. Your hurrying will avail you naught. I shall prompt the needful words without your mind's consent, and direct your organs of speech as justice and convenience require. I shall guide the reins of speech, and, though you understand it not, employ your tongue for each prophetic utterance (*Vit. Mos.* 1.274).

Within a few days, Balaam delivered his first oracle:

> He advanced outside, and straightway became possessed, and there fell upon him the truly prophetic spirit which banished utterly from his soul his art of wizardry. For the craft of the sorcerer and the inspiration of the Holiest might not live together. Then he returned, and, seeing the sacrifices and the altars flaming, he spake these oracles as one repeating the words which another had put into his mouth (*Vit. Mos.* 1.277).

These descriptions of Balaam's first oracle preserve traces of their biblical source: the angel's speech is an elaboration of Num 22:35; the reference to the prophetic spirit is traceable to Num 24:2; and the expression, "words . . . put into his mouth," echoes Num 23:5.

Far more evident, however, is the transformation which has taken place in Philo's version. The passivity implicit in Balaam's having said what he heard (Num 22:35) and having received a word in his mouth (Num 23:5) is elaborated with an exclamation point. For Philo, it entails the complete surrender of Balaam's mental faculties. The angel predicted that Balaam's mind would not be active during the oracle, and he did indeed understand nothing. Balaam did no more than repeat the words which were given to him: "he spake these oracles as one repeating the words which another had put into his mouth." This emphasis is evident further in Philo's interpretation of Balaam's second oracle. According to the biblical version, in Num 23:16, this oracle transpired when "the LORD put a word in his [Balaam's] mouth . . ." Philo expands this laconic description: "In this solitude, he was suddenly possessed, and, understanding nothing, his reason as it were roaming, uttered these prophetic words which were put into his mouth" (*Vit. Mos.* 1.283). Once again, the oracle transpired when Balaam's intellectual faculties were extinguished.

Josephus' narrative summary of Balaam's first oracle is uncommonly similar to Philo's portrayal of Balaam's experience: "Such was the inspired utterance of one who was no longer his own master but was overruled by the divine spirit to deliver it" (*Ant.* 4.118). In the context of the ensuing speech of Balaam, in which Balaam explained why he had blessed Israel, Josephus employs two statements, each followed by an explanation introduced by an explanatory "for" to specify the mode of inspiration to which Balaam was susceptible:

> Balak . . . hast thou reflected on the whole matter and thinkest thou that it rests with us at all to be silent or to speak on such themes as these, when we are possessed by the spirit of God? For that spirit gives utterance to such language and words as it will, whereof we are all unconscious (*Ant.* 4.119).

Balaam continued:

> But God is mightier than that determination of mine to do this favor; and wholly impotent are they who pretend to such foreknowledge of human affairs, drawn from their own breasts, as to refrain from speaking that which the Deity suggests and to violate His will. For nothing within us, once He has gained prior entry, is any more our own (*Ant.* 4.121).

This repetition suggests how emphatically Josephus wanted his readers to know that Balaam was not in himself (*Ant.* 4.118), that he became unconscious (4.119), and that

he was no longer in possession of his mental faculties
(4.121).

Philo's and Josephus' interpretations permit us to pin-
point with relative accuracy the nature of Balaam's
inspiration.

- Balaam's conscious mental faculties were rendered
  inactive by the invading presence of the angelic
  spirit.

- Balaam was "possessed" by this angelic spirit (*Vit.
  Mos.* 1.277, 283) which gained early entry into him
  (*Ant.* 4.121).

- From within, this divine spirit utilized Balaam's
  mouth to produce oracular words and sounds of
  its own choosing.

Where Numbers 22–24 is ambiguous—on the source of
Balaam's oracles—the versions of Philo and Josephus ring
with clarity: the divine angelic spirit was the source of
Balaam's oracles. Where Numbers 22–24 is vague—on the
process involved in the production of oracles—the versions
of Philo and Josephus are unambiguous: Balaam was rendered unconscious by this angelic spirit who ousted his
mental control and manipulated his vocal chords to bless
Israel. These developments are impressive both in terms of
their clarity and creativity.

Ecstasy and the Greco-Roman Era

How might we explain this gap between the ambiguity of
the biblical story and the clarity of these two first-century
Jewish interpreters? The writings of Plato based upon the
life and teachings of Socrates provide an important clue to
the answer to this question. Socrates' statement that the
loss of mental control is the central characteristic of
inspired utterance can be located in his discussion of
madness:

> . . . but in reality the greatest of blessings come to us through
> madness, when it is sent as a gift of the gods. For the proph-
> etess at Delphi and the priestesses at Dodona when they
> have been mad have conferred many splendid benefits
> upon Greece both in private and in public affairs, but few or
> none when they have been in their right minds . . . (*Phaedrus*
> 244A-B).

Socrates also describes the inspiration of the poet, who "is
unable ever to indite until he has been inspired and put out
of his senses, and his mind is no longer in him . . ." (*Ion*
534B). Composition of odes, dance songs, and verse are
uttered "not by art . . . but by divine influence." Therefore,

> God takes away the mind of these and uses them as his min-
> isters, just as he does soothsayers and godly seers, in order
> that we who hear them may know that it is not they who
> utter these words of great price, but that it is God himself
> who speaks and addresses us through them (*Ion* 534C-D).[5]

Discernible here is a repository of conceptions which lie at
the base of Philo's and Josephus' belief that Balaam suc-
cumbed to madness, to divine madness, which caused his
mind to wander, his consciousness to be lost.

Plato provides another piece of the scaffolding—this
time with respect to the role of figures of mediation—upon
which Philo and Josephus could build their presentation of
the angelic spirit which functions as the central mediator
figure in the story of Balaam. Plato describes a demonic
being—a demon—as:

> . . . interpreting and transporting human things to the gods
> and divine things to humans; entreaties and sacrifices from
> below, and ordinances and requitals from above: being mid-
> way between. It makes each supplement the other, so that
> the whole is combined in one. Through it are conveyed all
> divination and priestcraft concerning sacrifice and ritual
> and incantations, and all soothsaying and sorcery. God with
> man does not mingle: but the spiritual is the means of all
> society and converse of men with gods and of gods with
> men, whether waking or asleep . . . Many and multifarious
> are these spirits, and one of them is Love (*Symposium*
> 202E-203A).

The importance of this description of demons is evident in Philo's discussions of angels. In his most thorough explanation, *Gig.* 6–18 (on Gen 6:2), Philo introduces a comparison: "It is Moses' custom to give the name of angels to those whom other philosophers call demons . . . souls, that is, which fly and hover in the air" (*Gig.* 6). These angels are "consecrated and devoted to the service of the Father and Creator whose wont it is to employ them as ministers and helpers, to have charge and care of mortal man."

Although Plato provides the two elements of Balaam's experience—loss of mental control and an angelic or demonic being—he does not explicitly draw the sort of association between angels (demons) and loss of mental control that is integral to Philo's and Josephus's interpretation of Balaam. According to these two Greco-Roman Jewish authors, Balaam did not merely lose mental control. He lost the reins of his mental control to *an overpowering angelic spirit* which possessed him, thrust away his understanding, and utilized his vocal capacity to pronounce blessings upon Israel. For that association Plutarch's *De defectu oraculorum* is indispensable.

One of the participants in the discussion, Cleombrotus, attributes the decrease in oracular activity at Delphi to the departure of the mediating demons, what Philo would call angels. This is, Cleombrotus observes, a longstanding view that was claimed by adherents long in advance of himself:

> Let this statement be ventured for us, following the lead of many others before us, that coincidentally with the total defection of the guardian spirits assigned to the oracles and prophetic shrines, occurs the defection of the oracles themselves; and when the spirits flee or go to another place, the oracles themselves lose their power (*Def. Orac.* 418C-D).

Later in the discussion, Lamprias criticizes Cleombrotus' explanation, but before he does he summarizes it: "For what was said then [i.e., earlier], that when the demigods withdraw and forsake the oracles, these lie idle and inarticulate like the instruments of musicians . . ." (*Def. Orac.* 431A-B).

Although Philo, Josephus, and Cleombrotus are three quite different personalities, all three espouse a mode of inspiration in which an angelic or demonic being inspires oracular speech. This conclusion still does not exhaust the kinship of Cleombrotus' view with Philo's and Josephus' versions of Balaam. The *means* of inspiration are also analogous: the recipient of inspiration remains passive in the presence of the inspiring angel. Balaam, in Josephus' *Antiquities*, says, "For that spirit gives utterance to such language and words as it will, whereof we are all unconscious (4.120). In Philo's *De vita Mosis*, the angel predicts, "I shall prompt the needful words without your mind's consent" (1.274). In *De defectu oraculorum*, Cleombrotus accentuates this passivity by adopting the simile of musical instruments. When the demons return, "the oracles, like musical instruments, become articulate, since those who can put them to use are present and in charge of them" (*Def. Orac.* 418D). This image occurs as well in Philo's writings in a related description of the prophetic phenomenon. Philo equates the onset of ecstasy with the arrival of the divine spirit: "This is what regularly befalls the fellowship of the prophets. The mind is evicted at the arrival of the divine Spirit, but when that departs the mind returns to its tenancy" (*Her.* 265). Philo continues by connecting this interpretation of ecstasy in Gen 15:12 with the words: It was said to Abraham," in Gen 15:13:

> For indeed the prophet, even when he seems to be speaking, really holds his peace, and his organs of speech, mouth and tongue, are wholly in the employ of Another, to shew forth what He wills. Unseen by us that Other beats on the chords with the skill of a master-hand and makes them instruments of sweet music, laden with every harmony (*Her.* 266).

The ingredients of inspiration integral to Philo's version of Balaam—the spirit, an ecstatic state, the mutual exclusiveness of mortal and immortal, the prompting of the vocal organs, and the passivity of the prophet—coalesce in this definition of prophecy. The use here of the metaphor of music links this definition of prophecy to the view held by

Cleombrotus, according to which, "when the spirits return many years later, the oracles, like musical instruments, become articulate, since those who can put them to use are present and in charge of them" (*Def. Orac.* 418D).

Cleombrotus' explanation of Delphic inspiration, then, sheds extraordinary light on the interpretations of Philo and Josephus. All three preserve the boundaries between the spheres of gods and humans by attributing prophetic activity to an angelic or demonic being who plays upon a passive prophet. Still, Cleombrotus' point of view, despite its significance for understanding the views of Josephus and Philo, does not ultimately explain the inordinate emphasis they place upon the angel's manipulation of Balaam's vocal chords. According to Josephus, the angel "gives utterance to such language and words as it will . . ." (*Ant.* 4.120). According to Philo, the angel predicted: ". . . I shall prompt the needful words without your mind's consent, and direct your organs of speech as justice and convenience require. I shall guide the reins of speech, and, though you understand it not, employ your tongue for each prophetic utterance" (*Vit. Mos.* 1.274).

That the simile of the musician in Cleombrotus' interpretation does not adequately explain these detailed depictions of inspiration ought not to be surprising, for Cleombrotus' explanation is deemed inadequate even by some of his dialogue partners in *De defectu oraculorum*. Lamprias, for example, points out that Cleombrotus has not sufficiently explained the mechanics of inspiration. Rather, according to Lamprias, Cleombrotus' conviction "that when the demigods [demons] withdraw and forsake the oracles, these lie idle and inarticulate like the instruments of musicians"

> raises another question of greater import regarding the causative means and power which they employ to make the prophetic priests and priestesses possessed by inspiration and able to present their visions. For it is not possible to hold that the desertion by the demigods is the reason for the silence of the oracles unless we are convinced as to the manner in which the demigods, by having the oracles in their

charge and by their presence there, make them active and
articulate (*Def. Orac*. 431B).

Illumination of Philo's and Josephus' emphasis on the
manipulation of the vocal chords does not, however, lie far
afield of Cleombrotus' words. Earlier in *De defectu
oraculorum*, Lamprias maligned a view of inspiration according to which it could be imagined "that the god himself after
the manner of ventriloquists (who used to be called
'Eurycleis,' but now 'Pythones') enters into the bodies of his
prophets and prompts their utterances, employing their
mouths and voices as instruments" (*Def. Orac*. 414E). The
passivity of the prophet, according to this interpretation,
extends to the manipulation of his or her vocal chords. This
characterizes, of course, the experience of Balaam who
states, according to Josephus, that the "spirit gives utterance
to such language and words as it will" (*Ant.* 4.119), and to
whom, according to Philo, the angel promises that it will
"guide the reins of speech, and . . . employ your tongue for
each prophetic utterance" (*Vit. Mos.* 1.274).

Philo and Josephus adroitly adapt the two streams of
Greco-Roman conceptions of inspiration which were
maligned by Lamprias and espoused by Cleombrotus. This
combination of these views permits Philo and Josephus to
acknowledge the power of God in Balaam's oracles on
Israel's behalf while simultaneously maintaining God's distance from this diviner: not God but an angelic spirit possessed Balaam, took hold of his vocal chords, and mediated
oracles in praise of Israel.

The nature of Balaam's ecstasy in the versions of
Balaam proffered by Philo and Josephus can, therefore,
best be understood in the light of Plutarch's *De defectu
oraculorum*. Cleombrotus, a figure in this dialogue, both
attributes oracular activity to the presence of demonic
beings and implies, by means of the simile of musical
instruments, that such inspiration entails the loss of mental
control. This view alone shows how easily Philo and
Josephus attribute Balaam's oracles to an angelic spirit and
underscore his loss of mental control. The additional
detail, repeated in both versions, that the angel

manipulated Balaam's vocal chords, is discernible as well in Plutarch's *De defectu oraculorum*, in Lamprias' description of the gods' use of vocal chords.

Pseudo-Philo on the Ecstasy of Kenaz

The biblical book of Judges recounts briefly and colorlessly the exploits of a little-known judge named Othniel:

> But when the Israelites cried out to the LORD, the LORD raised up a deliverer for the Israelites, who delivered them, Othniel son of Kenaz, Caleb's younger brother. The spirit of the LORD came upon him, and he judged Israel; he went out to war, and the LORD gave King Cushan-rishathaim of Aram into his hand; and his hand prevailed over Cushan-rishathaim. So the land had rest forty years. Then Othniel son of Kenaz died (Judg 3:9–11).

One of the central figures in Pseudo-Philo's *Liber Antiquitatum Biblicarum* is Kenaz, Othniel's father. Pseudo-Philo has presumably substituted Kenaz for Othniel in his version. The role Kenaz takes on in *Liber Antiquitatum Biblicarum* is remarkable. His centrality is evident in the disparity between the meager mention Kenaz (biblical Othniel) receives in the biblical book of Judges and the immodest space he occupies in Pseudo-Philo's version. The effects of the spirit are attributed three times to this figure in *Liber Antiquitatum Biblicarum*. Twice the spirit is said to have inspired Kenaz to feats of mercurial heroism:

> And Kenaz arose, and the spirit of the LORD clothed him, and he drew his sword . . . (LAB 27:9).

> And when Kenaz heard their words, he was clothed with the spirit of power and was changed into another man, and he went down to the Amorite camp and began to strike them down (LAB 27:10).

Military success is not, however, the sole occasion for Kenaz's reception of the spirit; Pseudo-Philo spins, presumably out of equally thin air, a climactic prophetic vision at the end of Kenaz's extraordinary life:

> And when they [the prophets and elders of Israel] had sat down, [a] Holy Spirit came upon Kenaz and dwelled in him

and elevated his mind [put him in ecstasy], and he began to prophesy, saying . . . "Now I see what I had not hoped for, and I perceive that I did not understand . . ." (LAB 28:6)

Kenaz then recounts a vision of cosmic proportions which spans several millennia, from creation to judgment. This remarkable vision concludes:

> And when Kenaz had spoken these words, he was awakened, and his senses came back to him. But he did not know what he had said or what he had seen. But this alone he said to the people: "If the repose of the just after they have died is like this, we must die to the corruptible world so as not to see sins." And when he had said these words, Kenaz died and slept with his fathers. And the people mourned for him thirty days (LAB 28:10).

This depiction of Kenaz's reception of the spirit contains a great deal that does not arise from its biblical source, Judg 3:9–11. The scene in *Liber Antiquitatum Biblicarum* begins, first of all, with the observation that the spirit not only sprang upon Kenaz *but also* inhabited him. Neither conception—springing upon and indwelling—taken independently can be considered unbiblical. The verb, "leapt" (*insilire*), echoes 1 Samuel 10–11 rather than Judges 3; in the Vulgate of 1 Sam 10:6, 10, and 11:6, this verb depicts the powerful presence of the spirit when it overcame Saul, causing him to prophesy or to gather his people for war by cutting a yoke of oxen in several pieces. The notion of a spirit that indwells an individual is also at home in numerous texts that speak of wisdom, such as Gen 41:38, Exod 31:3, Num 27:18–20, Deut 34:9, Job 27:3, 32:7–8 and 18, and MT Dan 4:5–6, 4:15, 5:11–14. However, what distinguishes Kenaz's experience from these biblical texts is the juxtaposition of these two very different concepts of the spirit's advent: the spirit both sprang upon Kenaz *and* indwelt him.

Pseudo-Philo describes not only the mode of the spirit's presence, but also the effect which the spirit had upon Kenaz: the onset of ecstasy occurred when the spirit caused Kenaz's mind to ascend. The end of Kenaz's ecstatic experience transpired when ". . . he was awakened, and his sense came back to him." Kenaz was in a trance-like state from which it was necessary to awaken him. As if this were not adequate to call attention to the ecstatic character of Kenaz's vision, Pseudo-Philo records as well: "But he did not know what he had said or what he had seen" (LAB 28:10).

An extraordinarily rich coalescence of non-biblical details, therefore, serves to underscore the ecstatic nature of Kenaz's experience. The spirit springs upon Kenaz, indwells him, and elevates his mind just prior to his death. A vision ensues in which Kenaz's mind traverses the cosmos to see the judgment that will transpire far in the future. Once he is awakened and his mind returns from its travels, Kenaz is unable to recollect what he saw. The contours of the Holy Spirit's effect upon Kenaz are clear and well-conceived, and they are most decidedly *not* the contours supplied readily by the biblical story he purports to re-tell. These elements are, however, explicable within the Greco-Roman culture in which the *Liber Antiquitatum Biblicarum* was composed.[6]

Such extra-biblical elements correspond to popular Greco-Roman concepts of the ascent of the soul as they are detailed by Cicero in his *De divinatione*, which he composed during the first century BCE. In an illuminating summary of the inspired prophetic ascent of the soul, Quintus, Cicero's brother, and a chief proponent of the Stoic view of inspiration, says:

> When, therefore, the soul has been withdrawn by sleep from contact with sensual ties, then does it recall the past, comprehend the present, and foresee the future. For though the sleeping body then lies as if it were dead, yet the soul is alive and strong, and will be much more so after death when it is wholly free of the body. Hence its power to divine is much enhanced by the approach of death. For example, those in the grasp of a serious and fatal sickness realize the fact that death impends; and so, visions of dead people generally appear to them and then their desire for fame is strongest; while those who have lived otherwise than as they should, feel, at such a time, the keenest sorrow for their sins (*Div.* 1.63).

Following this summary, Quintus provides an example from Posidonius "of the power of dying people to prophesy" (1.64). Kenaz of the *Liber Antiquitatum Biblicarum* could equally provide another example of such an inspired figure. Just prior to his death, Kenaz enters a state akin to sleep, from which he must be awakened, when his *sensus* is elevated in a vision. Although Kenaz confesses that his eye does not know what it sees, his vision nonetheless extends from the abyss to the mountaintops and encompasses what he assumes is the entire seven thousand years of human existence. The chronological span of this vision, therefore, as in Cicero's summary, encompasses the creation (past) and the consummation (future) of the world, providing the basis for an exhortation to his hearers (present).

A similar description of inspired ascent from the first century CE is proffered by Plutarch who, in his interpretation of Plato's *Timaeus* 71E, contends that souls exercise their innate capacity "in dreams, and some in the hour of death, when the body becomes cleansed of all impurities and attains a temperament adapted to this end, a temperament through which the reasoning and thinking faculty of the souls is relaxed and released from their present state as they range amid the irrational and imaginative realms of the future" (*Def. Orac.* 432C). This description coincides with the experience of Kenaz, whose *sensus* is raised in a sleep-like state to range the future just prior to his death.

This coalescence of elements of inspiration suggests that the contours of Kenaz's visionary experience were shaped in a Jewish milieu which incorporated, consciously or unwittingly, fundamental elements of popular Greco-Roman views on the ascent of the soul. That Pseudo-Philo's portrait reflects *popular* rather than esoteric thinking on the subject is evident in a detail such as the need for Kenaz to be awakened. One of the interlocutors in Plutarch's *De genio Socratis*, Simmias, observes with disdain that, "In popular belief, on the other hand, it is only in sleep that people receive inspiration from on high; and the notion that they are so influenced when awake and in full possession of their faculties is accounted strange and incredible" (589D).[7]

These observations, illuminating though they be, do not adequately explain the totality of Pseudo-Philo's additions to Judg 3:9–11. To ascertain the contours of prophetic inspiration as it could be understood during Pseudo-Philo's era, we turn again to *De divinatione*, in which Cicero's brother, Quintus, describes the inspiration of Cassandra, "who prophesied . . . under a heaven-inspired excitement and exaltation of soul" (1.89). This thumbnail description of Cassandra's abilities presupposes a lengthier description in which she illustrates how the human soul's ability to foreknow the future can be abnormally developed:

> Therefore the human soul has an inherent power of presaging or of foreknowing infused into it from without, and made a part of it by the will of God. If that power is abnormally developed, it is called "frenzy" or "inspiration," which occurs when the soul withdraws itself from the body and is violently stimulated by a divine impulse (*Div.* 1.66).

In a later discussion of prophetic ecstasy, Quintus resumes the argument that, "In fact, the human soul never divines naturally, except when it is so unrestrained and free that it has absolutely no association with the body, as happens in the case of frenzy and of dreams" (*Div.* 1.113). He develops, on the basis of *Phaedrus* 246A-247E, the Platonic image of the ascent of the soul:

> Those then, whose souls, spurning their bodies, take wings and fly abroad—inflamed and aroused by a sort of passion—these . . . I say, certainly see the things which they foretell in their prophecies. Such souls do not cling to the body and are kindled by many different influences. For example, some are aroused by certain vocal tones, as by Phrygian songs, many by groves and forests, and many others by rivers and seas. I believe, too, that there were certain subterranean vapors which had the effect of inspiring persons to utter oracles (*Div.* 1.114).

Of this form of inspiration, the signal example is, once again, Cassandra, who illustrates the principle that "the frenzied soul sees the future long in advance . . ." (*Div.* 1.114).

Characteristic features of the prophetic experience can be garnered from Quintus' accounts of Cassandra:

- the ascent of the soul apart from the body;

- a frenzied condition of inflammation and excitement;

- the impetus of external arousal by a violent divine impulse or tones, forests, vapors, etc.;

- knowledge of the future.

These features reappear in less anecdotal and more philosophical form in Plutarch's *De defectu oraculorum*, in which Lamprias, another ardent proponent of Stoicism, explains Delphic inspiration in very similar terms. Like Quintus in Cicero's *De divinatione*, Lamprias shares the Stoic conviction that the soul's innate capacity to divine the future is hampered by its association with the body. When, however, the soul is free of the body's impurities and of mental control, it can range the realms of the future:

> Souls therefore, all possessed of this power, which is innate but dim and hardly manifest, nevertheless oftentimes disclose its flower and radiance in dreams, and some in the hour of death, when the body becomes cleansed of all impurities and attains a temperament adapted to this end, a temperament through which the reasoning and thinking faculty of the soul is relaxed and released from their present state as they range amid the irrational and imaginative realms of the future (*Def. Orac.* 432C).

The absence of mental control is so important that Lamprias reiterates the point that the condition of enthusiasm requires release from intellectual effort:

> But that which foretells the future, like a tablet without writing, is both irrational and indeterminate in itself, but receptive of impressions and presentiments through what may be done to it, and inconsequentially grasps at the future when it is farthest withdrawn from the present. Its withdrawal is

brought about by a temperament and disposition of the body as it is subjected to a change which we call inspiration (*Def. Orac.* 432C-D).

Lamprias continues by proffering examples of the catalysts which bring about this change in condition, opting himself for the final example:

> Often the body of itself alone attains this disposition. Moreover the earth sends forth for men streams of many other potencies, some of them producing derangements, diseases, or deaths; others helpful, benignant, and beneficial, as is plain from the experience of persons who have come upon them. But the prophetic current and breath is most divine and holy, whether it issue by itself through the air or come in the company of running waters; for when it is instilled into the body, it creates in souls an unaccustomed and unusual temperament, the peculiarity of which it is hard to describe with exactness . . . (*Def. Orac.* 432D-E).

This discussion of Delphic inspiration does not stand alone among Plutarch's writings. In a discussion indebted to Plato's enumeration of the four forms of madness (*Phaedrus* 265B), Plutarch delineates four kinds of inspiration. The second, he observes, entails the loss of mental control:

> There is a second kind, however, which does not exist without divine inspiration. It is not intrinsically generated but is, rather, an extrinsic afflatus that displaces the faculty of rational inference; it is created and set in motion by a higher power. This sort of madness bears the general name of "enthusiasm" (*Amatorius* 758E).

Such an explanation reveals that the Stoic interpretation of Delphic inspiration is actually anchored in a more general understanding of enthusiasm which can, in turn, be traced to Plato's discussion of madness.

What is indeed striking about Plutarch's explanations is that, though they rely far more on philosophical concepts and vocabulary—Cicero's is self-consciously more reliant upon illustrations (e.g., *Div.* 1.68)—they follow the same contours as Cicero's in their effort to explain the prophetic experience. Unifying features of these discussions of Cicero and Plutarch include:

- a soul that withdraws from the body and ranges amidst the realm of the future;

- a frenzied condition of inflammation and excitement, a hot and fiery soul;

- external arousal by a divine impulse, usually in the form of physical phenomena, of which the vapor of Delphi constitutes the best example;

- knowledge of the future.

In light of the different approaches employed by Cicero and Plutarch, the similarities between their discussions are astonishing, creating a conceptual umbrella of sorts, spanning the period from ca. 50 BCE to ca. 100 CE, during which time Pseudo-Philo probably composed his *Liber Antiquitatum Biblicarum*. In light of the popularity Stoicism experienced during the first century, as well as the fame of Delphi, the incorporation of these popular Stoic elements into Pseudo-Philo's rewritten Bible is hardly surprising. Each of these elements of popular Greco-Roman culture informs the depiction of Kenaz in *Liber Antiquitatum Biblicarum*: his mind (*sensus*) ascends to range the realms of the future when it is leapt upon and indwelt by the Holy Spirit; his experience cannot be remembered once he is awakened from the ecstatic state, although he has received a vivid vision of the future.

There remains one further element, introduced into the final lines of Kenaz's experience, which exhibits extraordinarily close affinities with Pseudo-Philo's Greco-Roman milieu: "But he did not know what he had said or what he had seen." This inability to remember cannot be explained by adducing biblical antecedents. Such an impact of inspiration was, on the other hand, integral to several accounts of oracular ecstasy during the Greco-Roman era and later.

The headwaters of this interpretation are Plato's *Apology* 22C and *Meno* 99C. In these passages, Plato contends that inspired poets do not know what they are saying. This view spawned interpretations in which the inability to recall what was experienced during a period without mental control underlined the authenticity of the prophetic condition.

As early as the late first or early second century CE, the pseudonymous Jewish author of 4 Ezra reveals an awareness of this interpretation in a description of an inspired experience in which Ezra allegedly dictated ninety-four books. During this period, Ezra's heart poured forth understanding, and wisdom increased in his breast *because* his own spirit retained its memory. The need to explain that Ezra retained his memory suggests that the author is aware of a form of inspiration that entailed the loss of memory (4 Ezra 14:40).[8]

The conviction that inspiration may bring a loss of recollection appears more explicitly in the writings of the second century CE public speaker and man of letters, Aelius Aristides. Following his defense of the Delphic priestesses of Apollo, Aelius Aristides discusses the inspiration of the priestesses of Zeus in Dodona, "who know as much as the God approves, and for as long as he approves." These inspired priestesses have no knowledge of Zeus' oracles prior to inspiration, "nor afterwards do they know anything which they have said, but all inquirers understand it better than they" (*In Defense of Oratory* 43).

The second- or third-century Christian author, Pseudo-Justinus, in his *Cohortatio ad Graecos*, discusses Plato's admiration for the Sibyl because her prophecies came to pass. To support his case, Ps-Justin paraphrases Plato's *Meno*, in which prophetic persons are said to be divine. Twice in this paraphrase, Ps-Justin expresses the opinion that the Sibyl cannot recall what she said while inspired:

> For, unlike the poets who, after their poems are penned, have power to correct and polish . . . she was filled indeed with prophecy at the time of the inspiration, but as soon as the inspiration ceased, there ceased also the remembrance of all she had said . . . (37.2).

... they said also that they who then took down her prophecies, being illiterate persons, often went quite astray from
the accuracy of the meters; and this, they said, was the cause
of the want of meter in some of the verses, the prophetess
having no remembrance of what she had said, after the possession and inspiration ceased, and the reporters having,
through their lack of education, failed to record the meters
with accuracy (37.3).[9]

This conviction concerning inspiration characterizes
as well a passage in the *Collationes* or Institutes for monastic
orders written by John Cassian, who lived during the late
fourth and early fifth centuries CE. In the context of a discussion of demon possession, he contrasts two types of possessed people, those who "are affected by them [demons]
in such a way as to have not the slightest conception of what
they do and say, while others know and afterwards recollect
it" (*Collationes* 12).[10]

The Christian prologue to the *Sibylline Oracles*, which
was composed no earlier than the end of the fifth century,
advances this same interpretation of Plato's view of prophetic inspiration in an effort to explain the occasional
absence of metrical accuracy. The author does not purport
to invent this explanation but appeals instead to the Christian apologist Lactantius[11] who, claims the author, "set forth
in his own works what had been said by the Sibyls about the
ineffable glory . . ." The author of the prologue explains:

When the Sibylline verses found with us can easily be
despised by those who are knowledgeable in Greek culture,
not only because they are easily available (for things which
are rare are thought valuable) but also because not all the
verses preserve metrical accuracy, he has a rather clear argument. This is the fault of the secretaries, who did not keep
pace with the flow of speech or even were ignorant, not of
the prophetess. For the memory of what had been said
ceased with the inspiration. With regard to this, even Plato
said that they describe many great things accurately while
knowing nothing of what they say" (*Sibylline Oracles* Prologue, 82–91).

Although Plato himself had not contended that authentic
inspiration entails an inability to remember, these

interpreters did. The persistence of this interpretation, spanning several centuries, is impressive, as is the variety of adherents to it: a late first or early second century CE Jewish author who claimed that Ezra did *not* lose the ability to remember his experience; an affluent second century Greco-Roman orator; a second-century Christian apologist; a fourth-century Christian monastic leader; and a Christian editor who "set forth the oracles called Sibylline, which are found scattered and confusedly read and recognized, in one continuous and connected book" (*Sibylline Oracles* prologue, 9–10). The diversity of these witnesses to a shared view of inspiration or possession with respect to recollection suggests that this was a popular, widely held view during the Greco-Roman era, during which period the *Liber Antiquitatum Biblicarum* was composed. Moreover, the persistent attribution of this interpretation to Plato, as well as the adherence of Aelius Aristides to this view, indicate a clear awareness that this belief about prophetic inspiration lay along a Greco-Roman trajectory.

Summary

What this brief analysis of interpretations of Numbers 22–24 and Judg 3:9–11 suggests is how creatively and deftly early Jewish authors could introduce the notion of ecstasy into their versions of biblical texts. According to Philo and Josephus, the spirit is an angel, a pre-eminent demonic being charged with the task of producing oracles through the misguided seer by conquering Balaam, ousting his mental control, and speaking by means of his vocal chords but without Balaam's consent or awareness. Pseudo-Philo also supplements the biblical text. While Judg 3:9–11 does not detail the effect of the spirit when it came upon Othniel, according to *Liber Antiquitatum Biblicarum*, Kenaz was transformed into a military leader (27:9–10) and, at the end of his life, became a visionary, with his mind elevated when the spirit leapt upon him and dwelt in him (28:6). He emerged from his ecstatic state unable to recall what he had spoken.

These interpretations suggest the range of repositories that were available to Jewish biblical interpreters during the Greco-Roman era. Each interpreter commences, of course, with the biblical text. Their versions of biblical stories, however, cannot be satisfactorily explained from biblical antecedents alone. Nor are Platonic antecedents adequate. It is rather Greco-Roman discussions of Delphic inspiration, such as we have discerned in the writings of Cicero and Plutarch, that prove adequate to explain the ease with which Philo, Josephus, and Pseudo-Philo import the experience of ecstasy into the biblical stories of Kenaz and Balaam.

3

The Inspired Interpretation of the Scholar

During the Greco-Roman era, the blessings of madness were believed to be plentiful. Cassandra may have cowered from "that bloody torch," but she recognized in this sudden rage the advent of a god.[1] The Delphic priestess may have reeled from the invasion of Apollo, but she was privy, unlike sober humans, to even more than she revealed.[2] The Jewish Sibyl may have lamented the lashing her spirit underwent, but she well knew that she divulged "unfailing truth . . . as much as God bids" her to say.[3] In this era, so transformative for Judaism and formative for Christianity, one could legitimately speak of "the blessings of madness."[4]

One could also have spoken of "the blessings of intellect." Simmias, in Plutarch's *De genio Socratis*, expresses undisguised disdain for the "popular belief" that people become inspired in sleep rather than when they are "awake and in full possession of their faculties." People who adhere to such false notions, claims Simmias, are themselves troubled, incapable of hearing the messages of demons which "find an echo in those only whose character is untroubled and soul unruffled" (*Gen. Socr.* 589D). The extent of Socrates' shadow during the Greco-Roman era, as well as a particular interest in his *daimonion*, attest to the vitality and persistence of discussions about the role of the intellect (*Gen. Socr.* 588D-E), about the pre-eminence of purity of soul (Cicero, *Div.* 1.122), and about the enviable possession of wisdom (Diogenes Laertius, *Lives of the Philosophers* 2.37; Philo, *Plant.* 65).

Jewish authors possessed within their own heritage, as well, a tradition that valued wisdom's treasures.[5] It is not, therefore, surprising that the process of interpreting those literary treasures should be associated with inspiration. The following early Jewish authors present in various forms the conviction that true interpretation was an inspired process, that faithful interpretation was a charismatic phenomenon that led to the sharpening rather than elimination—as in ecstasy—of the intellectual powers demanded of the interpreter.

Nehemiah

In an era of rebuilding and reflection following the return from exile in 530 BCE, authors began to glance sweepingly over the past and to summarize the work of the spirit. In the prayer of Ezra in Nehemiah 9, Ezra ascribes centuries of prophetic warning to the spirit: "Many years you were patient with them, and warned them by your spirit through your prophets; yet they would not listen. Therefore you handed them over to the peoples of the lands" (9:30).[6] Such an association of the spirit with the prophets, in the wake of the editing of the prophecies of the Isaiah corpus and Ezekiel, both of which amply connect prophecy with the spirit, is hardly surprising. But in the same prayer of Ezra occurs the less predictable conviction that God had given the spirit to the Israelites in the wilderness to instruct them: "You gave your good spirit to instruct them, and did not withhold your manna from their mouths, and gave them water for their thirst" (9:20).

This reference to the spirit is situated in the context of a prayer of confession which contains a lengthy retrospective, beginning with the creation of the heavens (9:6) and concluding with the exile (9:30). The immediate context of this reference to the spirit within this prayer is Neh 9:19–25, which extends from God's provisions in the wilderness to the gift of the land. This portion of Ezra's recounting of Israel's history corresponds to the prior section, Neh 9:12–15. These two parallel portions are divided by an account of Israelite rebellion (9:16–18). The reiteration of the elements of Neh 9:12–15 in Neh 9:19–25 is striking:

- the pillars of cloud and fire: 9:12 & 9:19

- good laws or instruction: 9:13–14 & 9:20a

- physical provision of
  manna and water: 9:15a & 9:20b-21

- promise and possession
  of the land: 9:15b & 9:22–25

The effect of this repetition is to produce a correspondence between the giving of Torah in the wilderness (9:13–14) and the giving of the spirit in the wilderness (9:20). Neh 9:13–14 recounts the giving of Torah at Sinai: "You came down also upon Mount Sinai, and spoke with them from heaven, and gave them right ordinances and true laws, good statutes and commandments, and you made known your holy Sabbath to them and gave them commandments and statutes and a law through your servant Moses." Its counterpart, Neh 9:20a, which is also bounded by references to the pillars of cloud and fire and the gift of manna and water, reads, "You gave your good spirit to instruct them . . ."

The nature of the relationship between Torah in 9:13–14 and spirit in 9:20 can be ascertained by means of the verb, "to instruct [them]" (9:20a). The Hebrew root, *śkl*, occurs earlier in Nehemiah 8, as both noun and verb, in conjunction with the interpretation of Torah. On the first day of the seventh month, "they read from the book, from the law of God, with interpretation. They gave *the sense*, so that the people understood the reading" (8:8). On the following day, "the heads of the ancestral houses of all the people, with the priests and the Levites, came together to the scribe Ezra in order *to study* the words of the law" (8:13).

The association of this verb and its cognate noun with the interpretation ("the sense" in 8:8) and study (8:13) of Torah in Nehemiah 8 suggests that the verb ought as well in Nehemiah 9 to denote instruction on the basis of Torah. If the occurrences of the root, *śkl*, in Nehemiah 8 be taken together with the parallel between Torah and spirit in Nehemiah 9, then the function of the spirit is patently to instruct on the basis of Torah. Alongside the gift of the Torah, then, came the gift of the good spirit for interpreting Torah.

Ben Sira

Centuries later, Ben Sira embraces a similar conception of inspired interpretation when he, in self-conscious reflection upon his own scribal calling, describes the wisdom of the scribe:

> If the Lord Almighty desires,
> he [the scribe] will be filled by a spirit of
>   understanding;
> he will pour out his own words of wisdom
> and by prayer he will give thanks to the Lord.
> He will direct his counsel and knowledge
> And he will reflect upon hidden matters.
> He will make known the instruction of what he has
>   learned
> and boast in the law of the covenant of the Lord.[7]

It is important to recognize that the filling of the spirit is not in this context associated principally with the interpretation of literary (e.g., biblical) texts. Rather, in the three lines which follow this reference to the spirit of wisdom, Ben Sira focuses, not upon texts to be interpreted, but upon his own abilities: his words; his prayer; his counsel and knowledge.

Nonetheless, the ensuing lines indicate that the scribe's instruction is not free floating but tethered to Torah, consisting of what he has learned from his study of the law of the covenant of the Lord. Moreover, the encomium on the scribe, of which this is a part, begins with three references to portions of the Hebrew Bible: the Torah (38:34); prophecies (39:1); and elements of wisdom literature, such as sayings, parables, and proverbs (39:2–3). The task of interpreting the Bible remains, therefore, within Ben Sira's purview when he focuses upon his own teaching abilities.

The description of the spirit as the "spirit *of understanding*" in Sir 39:6 is not insignificant because it intimates that Ben Sira regards interpretation and instruction as processes which require intellectual acumen. This impression is borne out by the context of this description, in which the scribe is the consummate scholar who preserves the sayings of famous people, cracks puzzling proverbs, and appears before foreign rulers in royal courts (39:2–5). The scribe discloses what he has ascertained through scholarly study (39:8a).

Furthermore, Ben Sira reveals a stubborn bias against ecstasy in his intolerance toward people who accept other forms of knowledge which are attained through divination, omens, and dreams, when he writes: "The senseless have vain and false hopes, and dreams give wings to fools. As one who catches at a shadow and pursues the wind, so is anyone who believes in dreams . . . Divinations and omens and dreams are unreal . . ." (34:1–2, 5a). Ben Sira casts his lot rather with those who choose instead the life of study: "For dreams have deceived many, and those who put their hope in them have perished. Without such deceptions, the law will be fulfilled, and wisdom is complete in the mouth of the faithful" (34:7–8). He praises in this regard the well-traveled, educated person who knows many things and learns from observing others (34:9), even as he extols, just prior to his reference to the spirit of understanding, the scribe who "travels in foreign lands and learns what is good and evil in the human lot" (39:4).

The occurrence of the phrase, spirit of understanding, in a context which praises the intellectual skills of the scribe, within a literary text composed by an author, himself a scribe, who regards dreams and divination as illicit sources of knowledge, is a clear indication that, for Ben

Sira, the spirit leads the mind intact to the sorts of interpretation which cause a scribe to become renowned (39:9–11).

Qumran

Valuable references can be located as well in the literature from Qumran, although insight into their views of inspired interpretation cannot be extracted directly from these texts because references to the spirit do not overlap directly references to interpretation. Overt references to inspired interpretation, therefore, contain only veiled references to the spirit, while references to the spirit contain but veiled references to inspired interpretation. These extraordinary texts are, nonetheless, sufficiently suggestive to warrant discussion.

Revealed interpretative insight lies at the heart of this Community. The initiates at Qumran are obligated to take an oath to follow the Torah of Moses *as it is interpreted by means of revelation at Qumran*, ". . . in compliance with all that has been revealed concerning it to the sons of Zadok, the priests who keep the covenant and interpret his will . . ." (1QS 5.9). More specifically, the central figure of Qumran is the Righteous Teacher, to whom, according to the *Commentary on Habakkuk*, "God has disclosed all the mysteries of the words of his servants, the prophets" (1QpHab 7.4).

For this Community, the spirit plays an integral role. Several references to the spirit occur in the psalms of the Community, some of which may have been composed by the famed Righteous Teacher. In particular, 1QH 20.11–13 associates the spirit with revelation:

> And I, the Instructor, have known you, my God,
> through the spirit which you gave to me,
> and I have listened loyally to your wonderful secret through your Holy Spirit.
> You have opened within me
> knowledge of the mystery of your wisdom,
> the source of your power . . .

The vocabulary of this psalm exhibits an intriguing colloca-
tion of words which reflects a context of study. The psalmist
refers to himself as *maskil*, a noun built from the same
verbal root, *śkl*, which we encountered in Neh 8:8, 13 and
9:20 to describe both the instruction given by the scribal
leaders in the period of restoration and the function of the
good spirit. Further, the description of the spirit as that which
is placed within a person echoes Ezek 11:19, 36:26–27 and
37:14.[8] The first two of these references in Ezekiel associate
the gift of the spirit with obedience to Torah:

> I will give them one heart, and put a new spirit within them;
> I will remove the heart of stone from their flesh and give
> them a heart of flesh, so that they may follow my statutes
> and keep my ordinances and obey them. Then they shall be
> my people, and I will be their God (11:19–20).

> A new heart I will give you, and a new spirit I will put within
> you; and I will remove from your body the heart of stone
> and give you a heart of flesh. I will put my spirit within you,
> and make you follow my statutes and be careful to observe
> my ordinances (36:26–27).

It would be unjustifiable to wring from these texts an
explicit association between the spirit and interpretation.
Indeed, the absence of such explicit affirmations is significant in light of how readily the author of the *Community
Rule*, in contrast, attributes ancient prophetic revelation to
the Holy Spirit (1QS 8.15). Nonetheless, for this Community, so steeped in the biblical tradition that truth cannot be
conceived of without recourse to biblical conceptions and
phraseology—the Community in which the Holy Spirit can
be a means of knowing God and God's mysteries (1QH
20.11–13), the Community whose initiates are obligated to
follow Torah as it is interpreted peculiarly by its priestly
leaders (1QS 5.9), the Community whose central figure
receives divine aid to interpret prophetic texts (1QpHab
7.4)—for this Community, it is not difficult to envisage that
biblical interpretation by authorized, learned leaders was
indeed attributed to the spirit.[9]

Philo Judaeus

Inspired Insight

In Exod 16:22, it is told that the Israelites gathered twice as much manna as on prior days. Although such an action violates Moses' command to collect only their daily portion of manna (Exod 16:20–21), Moses connected it with the Sabbath and thus allowed a double portion to be gathered (16:22–23). Philo modifies this story by writing instead that God actually gave twice the usual amount—thus Israel did not violate a prior command. According to Philo, then,

> the shower of food from the air was less on the first days, but on a later day was doubled; and on those first days anything left melted and was dissolved till, after turning completely into moisture, it disappeared; but on that later day it admitted no change and remained just as it had been (*Vit. Mos.* 2.264).

Moses' response to this sign constitutes an inspired prediction of the Sabbath. In *Vit. Mos.* 2.264–65, Philo pinpoints precisely how this inspiration transpired:

> Moses, when he heard of this [the manna] and also actually saw it, was awestruck and, guided by what was not so much surmise as God-sent inspiration, made announcement of the Sabbath. I need hardly say that conjectures of this kind are closely akin to prophecies. For the mind could not have made so straight an aim if there was not also the divine spirit guiding it to the truth itself.

Philo's explanation understands the *mind* to be the focal point of the spirit's activity, *truth* to be the goal of the spirit's inspiration, and *conjecture* and *guidance* to be the methods of the spirit's activity. Alongside references to the mind and the truth, these two words, conjecture and guide, explain the powerful way in which the spirit inspires the mind to ascertain the truth.

Philo consistently employs the word *conjecture* in contexts that have to do with thought, opinions, and guessing. In *Gaius* 21, for example, Philo observes, "The human mind in its blindness does not perceive its real interest and all it can do is to take conjecture and guesswork for its guide instead of knowledge." He includes conjecture alongside human ideas, purposes, and aims (*Post. Cain* 80), and describes it as "second to the true vision . . . conjecture and theorizing and all that can be brought into the category of reasonable probability" (*Spec. Leg.* 1.38).[10]

Philo corroborates this interpretation of the inspiration of the conscious mind by employing the verb *guide* which occurs without exception in Philo's writings in association with the path toward virtue. Guides in the ascent to virtue include love of wisdom (*Opif.* 70) or divine reason (*Immut.* 182). When Philo describes wisdom itself as a guide, he presents the essential role of the conscious mind with exceptional clarity: "The mind is cleansed by wisdom and the truths of wisdom's teaching which guide its steps to the contemplation of the universe and all that is therein, and by the sacred company of the other virtues and by the practice of them shewn in noble and highly praiseworthy actions" (*Spec. Leg.* 1.269). The road to virtue is therefore concomitant with the purification of the mind. Philo's use of these two words, *conjecture* and *guide*, to explain Moses' ability to predict the future betokens a view of inspiration in which the highest achievement of human thought is attributable to the spirit.

The model for this form of inspiration may be traced to Socrates, whose memory cut a large swath through the philosophical reflection of the Greco-Roman era. Diogenes Laertius quotes the words of the Pythian priestess, "Of all people living Socrates is most wise," and adds himself that "for this he was most envied" (2.37). Philo depicts Socrates as "one who was enraptured by the beauty of wisdom" (*Plant.* 65), and Josephus ridicules his opponent, Apion, for including himself alongside renowned philosophers, "Socrates, Zeno, Cleanthes, and others of that caliber" (*CA* 2.135).

Of particular interest was the nature of Socrates' inspiring *daimonion*, which Plato consistently designated *to daimonion* (*Euthyphro* 3B; *Apologia* 40A) or, "something divine and demonic" (*Apologia* 31D). Socrates associated it with a sign (*Phaedrus* 242C; *Euthydemus* 272E) and reflected

". . . I thought I heard a voice from it . . ." (*Phaedrus* 242C). Philosophers including Xenophon (*Memorabilia* 1.1.2–5), the author of the pseudo-Platonic dialogue *Theages* (128D-29D), Cicero (*De divinatione* 1.122, 124), Maximus of Tyre (eighth *Exhortation*), and Diogenes Laertius (*Lives of the Philosophers* 2.32) devoted serious attention to the nature of Socrates' *daimonion* for more than half a millennium. Josephus belongs to this current of thought when he attributes Socrates' death to his claim "that he received communications from a certain demon . . ." (*CA* 2.263–64).[11]

Naturally the nature of Socrates' *daimonion* holds intense interest for Plutarch, who devotes two substantive discussions in his *De genio Socratis* to the nature and function of this demonic sign (580B–82C and 588B–89F). These conversations begin with a question raised by Theocritus:

> . . . but what, my dear sir, do we call Socrates' demon [sign]? For my part, nothing reported of Pythagoras' skill in divination has struck me as so great or so divine; for exactly as Homer has represented Athena as "standing at" Odysseus' "side in all his labors," so heaven seems to have attached to Socrates from his earliest years as his guide in life a vision of this kind, which alone "Showed him the way, illumining his path," in matters dark and inscrutable to human wisdom, through the frequent concordance of the inspiring demon with his own decisions (*Gen. Socr.* 580C).

Certain elements in this concept of inspiration are similar to Philo's description of communication from the spirit in *Vit. Mos.* 2.265. Theocritus understands the *daimonion* to be a guide; Philo uses the cognate verb, to guide, to describe the guidance of the divine spirit in *Vit. Mos.* 2.265. Further, the primary function of Socrates' *daimonion* in this introduction corresponds to the primary function of inspiration in the introduction to Philo's treatment of Moses' prophetic gift in *Vit. Mos.* 2.187–292, of which *Vit. Mos.* 2.265 is an illustration. The *daimonion* illumined matters inscrutable to human wisdom; Moses as prophet was to "declare by inspiration what cannot be apprehended by reason" (2.187). The parallel between Plutarch's portrayal of Socrates and Philo's depiction of Moses is impressive. As the *daimonion* was a guide to Socrates, inspiring him to comprehend inscrutable matters, so did the spirit guide Moses to comprehend truth otherwise unknowable.

The conversation in *De genio Socratis* does not conclude with this query and initial response. After a lengthy interruption, it returns to "the problem of the nature and mode of operation of the so-called sign of Socrates" (588B). Another of the dialogue participants, Simmias, proffers his own explanation of Socrates' peculiar form of inspiration: "Socrates . . . had an understanding which, being pure and free from passion, and commingling with the body but little, for necessary ends, was so sensitive and delicate as to respond at once to what reached him. What reached him, one would conjecture, was not spoken language, but the unuttered words of a demon, making voiceless contact with his intelligence by their sense alone" (588D–E).

This lucid explanation contains two elements of a concept of inspiration which prove extraordinarily illuminating for the interpretation of the spirit in the writings of Philo. First, the *daimonion* is not taken to mean, as it could be, merely anything divine, such as a sign (e.g., entrails, birds, or clouds), but as a demonic being. Simmias refers to this demon subsequently as a "higher power" (588E) and "a higher understanding and a diviner soul" (589B). Second, the process of inspiration consists of voiceless contact with the intelligence of brilliant people. Simmias elaborates this as well when he twice states that this higher power can "lead" the human soul (588E) or understanding (589B). Such guidance is possible because the thoughts of these "demons are luminous and shed their light on the demonic person [understood in an unequivocally positive sense as the 'spiritual' person]" (589B).

The correspondence between this concept of Socrates' inspiration and Philo's explanation of Moses' inspiration should not surprise us if we recollect that Philo frequently adopts Greco-Roman concepts of inspiration to elucidate and expand biblical accounts. He adopts Platonic vocabulary to explain the prophetic phenomenon. He portrays Balaam's inspiration as a form of ventriloquism in which a demonic (i.e., angelic) spirit takes control of Balaam's vocal chords. It is consistent with his exegetical tendencies to explain Moses' inspiration via Greco-Roman conceptions of inspiration. Further, the reader is not left to guess in *Vit. Mos.* 2.265 whether Philo has assimilated Greco-Roman conceptions, for he does so in *a narrative aside* that is clearly intended to explain Moses' experience in a manner that is comprehensible to his first-century Greco-Roman readers—"I need hardly say that . . ." Little wonder, then, that Moses and Socrates experience similar forms of inspiration:

> . . . the intelligence of the higher power guides the gifted soul . . . (Plutarch, *Gen Socr.* 588E).

> . . . the understanding may be guided by a higher understanding and a diviner soul . . . (Plutarch, *Gen. Socr.* 589B).

> . . . the divine spirit guiding it [the mind] to the truth itself (Philo, *Vit. Mos.* 2.265).

We have seen the enormous exegetical care Philo exercised to identify the divine spirit with the angel of Numbers 22–24 in the tale of Balaam. We noted, furthermore, the effort he expends to identify the "demons" of the Greek philosophers with the "angels" of Moses. Entirely consistent with these interpretative movements, and perfectly understandable in light of the hefty value placed upon the figure of Socrates in Philo's world, is his ready embrace of concepts and vocabulary associated with Socrates' *daimonion* in order to elucidate forms of inspiration that are left inchoate in the biblical story of Moses.

Inspired Interpretation

Philo applies a similar model of inspiration by the divine spirit to his own inspired ability to interpret the scriptures. In *Som.* 2.252, Philo describes the invisible voice which he customarily hears: "I hear once more the voice of the invisible spirit, the familiar secret tenant, saying, 'Friend, it would seem that there is a matter great and precious of which thou knowest nothing, and this I will ungrudgingly shew thee, for many other well-timed lessons have I given thee.'" This rare autobiographical reflection exhibits two characteristics of Moses' prophetic experience, as Philo describes it in *Vit. Mos.* 2.265: the spirit as the essential factor in leading to knowledge that is otherwise unknowable; and the conscious mind, which the spirit teaches. The occasion for inspiration is not, with Moses, the perception of the manna, but a specific point of interpretation—in this instance, the meaning of the name, Jerusalem.

Cher. 27–29 recounts a similar experience of inspiration in which Philo claims to receive a specific biblical interpretation. As in *Som.* 2.252, Philo again permits us a glimpse of his experience, when he discusses the "higher word"—the allegorical meaning—of the two Cherubim:

> But there is a higher thought than these. It comes from a voice in my own soul, which oftentimes is god-possessed and divines where it does not know. This thought I will record in words if I can. The voice told me that while God is indeed one, his highest and chiefest powers are two, even goodness and sovereignty ... O then, my mind, admit the image unalloyed of the two Cherubim, that having learnt its clear lesson of the sovereignty, and beneficence of the Cause, thou mayest reap the fruits of a happy lot. For straightway thou shalt understand how these unmixed potencies are mingled and united, how, where God is good, yet the glory of His sovereignty is seen amid the beneficence, how, where He is sovereign, through the sovereignty the beneficence still appears. Thus thou mayest gain the virtues begotten of these potencies, a cheerful courage and a reverent awe towards God.

Like *Som.* 2.252, *Cher.* 27–29 describes an experience of inspiration that leads to the solution of a similar exegetical conundrum. In *Cher.* 27–29, the question concerns why there are two Cherubim; in *Som.* 2.252, the question concerns why two different names are given for Jerusalem. That inspiration, moreover, is directed in *Cher.* 27–29, as in *Som.* 2.252, to the mind: "O then, my mind, admit the image unalloyed of the two Cherubim ..." The process is, once again, one of learning; as in *Som.* 2.252, so in *Cher.* 27–29 does the word, learn (*anadidaskein*), occur; Philo

claims to have "learnt its [the two Cherubim] clear lesson of
the sovereignty and beneficence of the Cause . . ." With
these related autobiographical reflections, Philo paints a
vivid picture of his inspired experiences as interpreter of
Torah. In both, Philo hears an external reality—voice or
spirit—which teaches his mind from within, leading it to
knowledge to which it would otherwise not attain.

Philo's reflections on the voice which prompts him to
solve exegetical difficulties (*Cher.* 27–29; *Som.* 2.252) have
their closest affinities with discussions of Socrates' *daimonion*
in Plutarch's *De genio Socratis*. Simmias expresses initially what
he claims often to have heard Socrates say, "that people who
laid claim to visual communication with Heaven were
imposters, while to such as affirmed that they had heard a
voice he paid close attention and earnestly inquired after the
particulars" (588C). Simmias conjectures further "that
Socrates' sign was perhaps no vision, but rather the perception of a voice or else the mental apprehension of language,
that reached him in some strange way" (588D), and that
"what reached him, one would conjecture, was not spoken
language, but the unuttered words of a demon, making
voiceless contact with his intelligence by their sense alone"
(588E). A voice (588C), a voice perceived by the pure mind
(588D), by intelligence (588E), the words of demons
(589D)—this is what Socrates comprehended. Philo claims
as well to hear a voice, not a physical voice heard from without, but a voice heard from within, which leads him to interpret Torah. The "higher thought" of Torah, claims Philo,
"comes from a voice in my own soul" (*Cher.* 27); the solutions
to exegetical difficulties arise when "the invisible spirit, the
familiar secret tenant" speaks (*Som.* 2.252).

Simmias explains further in *De genio Socratis* that only
extraordinary people in an intellectually alert condition
are capable of hearing this unspoken language:

> . . . the messages of demons pass through all other people,
> but find an echo in those only whose character is untroubled
> and soul unruffled, the very people in fact we call holy and
> demonic. In popular belief, on the other hand, it is only in
> sleep that people receive inspiration from on high; and the

notion that they are so influenced when awake and in full possession of their faculties is accounted strange and incredible. This is like supposing that a musician uses his lyre when the strings are slack, but does not touch or play it when it has been adjusted to a scale and attuned (*Gen. Socr.* 589D).

This lucid description of inspiration contains significant concepts which Philo appears to adopt in the laconic language of *Som.* 2.252. Philo describes the preparedness of his mind as free from faction and *turmoil*. Plutarch contends similarly that, in contrast to the ignorant masses, whose souls are in *turmoil* (*Gen. Socr.* 589E), demonic language can only be heard by those whose souls are untroubled and unruffled. Philo also describes laconically the process by which the divine spirit speaks as an echo. This reflects the predominant image employed by Plutarch to explain how the language of demons is communicated: the "messages of demons pass through all other people, but find an echo in those only whose character is untroubled and soul unruffled."

These correspondences between Philo's concept of the spirit and Socrates' demon are anchored by Philo's use of the word, "customary," in *Som.* 2.252 to describe the recurrent presence of the spirit, for this word constitutes an allusion to this key word in Plato's description of Socrates' demon.[12] Socrates refers to "the customary prophetic inspiration of the demon" (*Apologia* 40A), "the demonic and customary sign" (*Phaedrus* 242B), and "my customary demonic sign" (*Euthydemus* 272E). Socrates claims to have had this voice from his childhood (*Apologia* 31D), a contention which both the author of *Theages* (128D) and Plutarch (*Gen. Socr.* 580C; 589E-F) confirm.

The affinities between Socrates' demon and Philo's spirit are striking. Even as the ultimate source of Socrates' voice was a demon who customarily communicated to him because its unspoken language echoed within his untroubled soul, so the ultimate source of Philo's exegetical insight is the divine spirit which customarily communicates to him by echoing within his untroubled soul.

4 Ezra

We now turn to a major Jewish apocalypse. The author of
4 Ezra responded to the destruction of Jerusalem by cloak-
ing his views in the guise of Ezra the scribe. Ezra in 4 Ezra
receives the Holy Spirit not so much to interpret as to
re-write the twenty-four books of the Hebrew Bible which
were destroyed in 70 CE and to dictate an additional seventy books (4 Ezra 14:45–46). Because it is so rich in detail
and so lucidly written, 4 Ezra 14 opens an extraordinary
window into early Jewish concepts of inspiration toward
the conclusion of the first century CE. The account of Ezra's
inspired scribal experience begins with a bold request for
the Holy Spirit:

> For the world lies in darkness, and its inhabitants are with-
> out light. For your Law has been burned, and so no one
> knows the things which have been done or will be done by
> you. If then I have found favor before you, send the Holy
> Spirit to me, and I will write everything that has happened
> in the world from the beginning, the things which were writ-
> ten in your Law, that men may be able to find the path, and
> that those who wish to live in the last days may live
> (14:21–22).

God responds with alacrity to this request, commanding
Ezra to isolate himself for forty days from the people:

> But prepare for yourself many writing tablets, and take with
> you Sarea, Dabria, Selemia, Ethanus, and Asiel—these five,
> because they are trained to write rapidly; and you shall
> come here, and I will light in your heart the lamp of under-
> standing, which shall not be put out until what you are about
> to write is finished. And when you have finished, some
> things you shall make public, and some you shall deliver in
> secret to the wise; tomorrow at this hour you shall begin to
> write (14:24–26).

The promise of the lamp of understanding and the prediction that it will remain lit for the duration of Ezra's experience prepares him for an experience of inspiration in
which Ezra's mind will remain intact from beginning to
end. The nature of this experience, in which Ezra remains
intellectually aware, may be contrasted with Ezra's earlier

response to the vision of the heavenly Jerusalem: "I lay there like a corpse and I was deprived of my understanding. Then he [the angel] grasped my right hand and strengthened me and set me on my feet, and said to me, 'What is the matter with you? And why are you troubled? And why are your understanding and the thoughts of your mind troubled?'" (10:30–31). Ezra here has lost control of himself, not only physically but also mentally. He, his heart, and his mind are troubled. Ezra's moribund, uncomprehending state in this passage is fundamentally different from Ezra's experience of inspired writing in 4 Ezra 14, during which he proceeds energetically for forty days and nights with the lamp of understanding burning continually. His mind, in the former instance eclipsed, is in the latter sharpened.

The heightening of Ezra's intellectual abilities finds its most vivid expression in Ezra's own account of his experience:

> I took the five men, as he commanded me, and we proceeded to the field, and remained there. And on the next day, behold, a voice called me, saying, "Ezra, open your mouth and drink what I give you to drink." Then I opened my mouth, and behold, a full cup was offered to me; it was full of something like water, but its color was fire. And I took it and drank; and when I had drunk it, my heart poured forth understanding, and wisdom increased in my breast, for my spirit retained its memory; and my mouth was opened, and was no longer closed. And the Most High gave understanding to the five men, and by turns they wrote what was dictated, in characters which they did not know. They sat forty days, and wrote during the daytime, and ate their bread at night. So during the forty days ninety-four books were written (14:37–44).

Ezra's experience as the quintessential scribe, the tradent of wisdom, fulfills God's original promise that the lamp of understanding would burn without interruption. At the initial moment of his experience, as soon as Ezra drank the cup given to him, his heart poured forth understanding, and wisdom increased within him. This experience is comparable to Ben Sira's description of the scribal experience:

"he will be filled with the spirit of understanding; he will pour forth words of wisdom of his own" (Sir 39:6).

The author's emphasis upon the gushing of understanding and wisdom finds its climactic expression in the concluding description of the books Ezra dictated— a description which comprises as well the climactic conclusion of the entirety of 4 Ezra. Here the highest concentration of concepts in the entire book of 4 Ezra encapsulates the grandest attainment of the scribal tradition: "For in them [the ninety-four books] is the spring of understanding, the fountain of wisdom, and the river of knowledge" (14:47). From beginning to end, therefore, Ezra's scribal ability is heightened: the lamp of understanding remains lit; the drink initiates a pouring forth of Ezra's understanding and an increase in his wisdom; the product of this inspired experience is ninety-four books, which are themselves springs, fountains, and rivers of understanding, wisdom, and knowledge.

Another indication that Ezra's achievement was due to the heightening rather than displacement of his intellectual powers by the Holy Spirit is evident in the rationale the author gives for Ezra's increased understanding and wisdom. Ezra poured forth understanding and wisdom increased in his breast *because* his own spirit retained its memory. Loss of memory, we may recall, during the Greco-Roman era and later was a distinguishing mark of ecstasy which was included in the literature of Pseudo-Philo (LAB 28:10 and 62:2), Aelius Aristides, Pseudo-Justinus, John Cassian, and the author of the late prologue to the *Sybilline Oracles*. The assertion of the author of 4 Ezra, that Ezra's experience entailed the retention rather than loss of memory, distinguishes Ezra's experience of inspiration from the inspired ecstasy of prophets and seers.

This vivid and colorful first-century depiction of Ezra's inspired scribal activity, with its bold strokes that depict Ezra and his literary output as the highest attainment of understanding, knowledge, and wisdom, with the detail that Ezra retained his memory and thus did not succumb to ecstasy, and with the attribution of this experience to the

Holy Spirit, brings us full circle to Neh 9:20, the text with which our exploration of inspired interpretation began. Through literary parallels and the recurrence of the Hebrew root, *śkl*, the author of Nehemiah subtly, but unmistakably, associates the spirit with the scribal activity of interpreting Torah. The figure at the center of that evocative association was none other than Ezra: he brought the book of the law of Moses before the assembly (Neh 8:2); he read from it (8:3); Nehemiah, he, and the Levites taught the people on the first day (8:9); on the second day the heads of the ancestral houses, the priests, and the Levites came together to the scribe Ezra to study (root, *śkl*) Torah (8:13); and the prayer which contains the words, "You gave your good spirit to instruct them . . ." is uttered by Ezra (9:6). That implicit attribution of Ezra's scribal abilities to the good spirit was permutated in the late first century CE into an explicit request for the Holy Spirit and the consequent gift of understanding to Ezra, who poured forth understanding, increased in wisdom, retained his memory, and kept five qualified scribes occupied by dictating, within the compass of forty days, ninety-four books which represent the product of a remarkable combination of divine revelation and human intellect.

Summary

Many Jewish communities during the Greco-Roman era valued Torah and treasured their literary traditions, although they stood at a distance for a variety of reasons from the Temple in Jerusalem: for the author of Nehemiah and for Ben Sira the Temple was hardly as impressive as the Solomonic building; the devotees of Torah at Qumran repudiated the Temple; Philo lived in Alexandrian Egypt, far from that Temple; and the author of 4 Ezra wrote in the wake of the Temple's destruction. For these scholars, their literature would be possessed of peculiar significance. Little wonder, then, that they claimed, alongside the inspiration of biblical texts themselves, a form of inspiration that aided them in their own interpretation of their scriptures.

What all of these claimed in common, with varying degrees of specificity, was that their minds, under the inspiration of the divine spirit, could grasp realities and truths that were otherwise unknowable. Unlike the experience of ecstasy, these experiences of charismatic interpretation would transpire when human minds grew stronger rather than weaker, when intellect became more tenacious rather than tentative.

4 Conclusion
The Span of the Spirit

Among the insights that have risen to the surface of this analysis is the recognition that the divine spirit was accorded a remarkable breadth of impact by Jews after the exile. Its *effects* extended from ecstasy, with a loss of consciousness, to inspired interpretation, with a sharpening of intellect. Its *nature* could encompass an angelic being, such as in the Balaam tale according to Philo and Josephus and in Philo's recollection of his "customary friend," or a draught to be drunk, as in 4 Ezra. Its *recipients* extended from a diabolical foreign seer and seducer of Israel, Balaam, to quintessential scribes, the faithful tradents of Israelite tradition, such as Ben Sira and Ezra in 4 Ezra. Its *geographical ubiquity* was equally extensive, encompassing the various borders of the Mediterranean Sea, from Palestine in the east (Nehemiah, Ben Sira, *Liber Antiquitatum Biblicarum*, the Dead Sea Scrolls, and possibly 4 Ezra) to Alexandria in the south (Philo) to Rome in the north (Josephus).

In this book, then, I have tried to give an impression of the span of the spirit's impact. What is surprising is how easily the literary texts have lent themselves to illustrating that span despite the very narrow foci I chose: the inspired ecstasy of the seer and the inspired interpretation of the scholar. The foci represented by the title, *Of Two Minds*, constitute but a slender thread in a tapestry whose textures encompass far more than ecstasy and interpretation. To dispel the impression that the spirit's impact was limited to ecstasy and interpretation, therefore, I conclude this analysis with a pastiche of early Jewish texts that demonstrate how much more widely the effects of the spirit were believed by Jews of the Greco-Roman era to extend.

Creation

To begin at the beginning—the spirit is associated in a variety of ways with creation. The influence of Gen 1:2 is apparent in 2 Bar 21:4, in Baruch's address to God, ". . . you who created the earth, the one who fixed the firmament by the word and fastened the height of heaven by the spirit . . ." God responds to this prayer in 23:5, "For my spirit creates the living . . ." Ezra in 4 Ezra 6:39 similarly recalls the earliest creative activity of God: "And then the Spirit was hovering, and darkness and silence embraced everything; the sound of a human voice was not yet there. Then you commanded that a ray of light be brought forth . . ." In Judith 16:14, it is Gen 2:7 and 2:22, mediated through Ps 104:29–30, which influences the depiction of the spirit's relation to creation. Judith praises God,

> Let all your creatures serve you
> for you spoke, and they were made
> You sent forth your spirit, and it formed them
> there is none that can resist your voice.

The spirit's function vis-à-vis creation is not only to grant life but also to convict wrongdoers. A representative of the Alexandrian wisdom tradition can contend that the ungodly will be punished "because the spirit of the Lord has filled the world, and that which holds all things together knows what is said" (WisSol 1:7). In the words of the Sibyl, composed by another Egyptian author,

> The earth itself will also drink
>   of the blood of the dying;
> wild beasts will be sated with flesh.
> God himself, the great eternal one, told me
>   to prophesy all these things.
> These things will not go unfulfilled.
> Nor is anything left unaccomplished that he so much
>   as puts in mind
> for the spirit of God which knows no falsehood is
>   throughout the world (*Sibylline Oracles* 3.696–701).

Prophecy

We have analyzed in some depth the prophetic abilities of biblical figures such as Balaam, Kenaz, and Moses throughout this book. There are as well many other references to spirit-inspired prophecy which do not necessarily detail the process of inspiration (e.g., ecstasy in the cases of Balaam and Kenaz, intellectual acuity in the case of Moses). According to *Jubilees*, for example, "a spirit of truth descended upon the mouth" of Rebecca so that she could bless her children (25:14), and Jacob blessed Levi and Judah when "a spirit of prophecy came down upon his mouth" (31:11). A section of the Enoch cycle of literature begins when Enoch commands, "Now, my son Methuselah, (please) summon all your brothers on my behalf, and gather together to me all the sons of your mother; for a voice calls me, and the spirit is poured over me so that I may show you everything that shall happen to you forever" (*1 Enoch* 91:1). In a humorous portion of the Testament of Abraham, in which the archangel Michael cannot find the resources to convince Abraham that he will die, God says to Michael: "And I shall send my Holy Spirit upon his son Isaac, and I shall thrust the mention of his death into Isaac's heart, so that he will see his father's death in a dream" (TAbr [A] 4:8).

This association between the spirit and prophecy is evident as well with respect to figures other than Kenaz in *Liber Antiquitatum Biblicarum*. The spirit comes upon Miriam as the recipient of a dream in which the birth of Moses is predicted (LAB 9:10), and Deborah is said explicitly to have predicted Sisera's demise by the inspiration of the spirit (LAB 31:9). In a recasting of Deut 34:9, the explicit biblical reference to the spirit of wisdom is thoughtfully supplanted by allusions to 1 Sam 10:6 and Judg 6:34—other biblical texts which refer to the spirit—and followed by a prophetic utterance of Joshua (LAB 20:2–3).

> Then God said to Joshua the son of Nun, "Why do you mourn and why do you hope in vain that Moses yet lives? Why do you wait to no purpose, because Moses is dead. Take

his garments of wisdom and clothe yourself, and with his belt of knowledge gird your loins, and you will be changed and become another man . . ." And Joshua took the garments of wisdom and clothed himself and girded his loins with the belt of understanding. And when he clothed himself with it, his mind was afire and his spirit was moved, and he said to the people . . .

Even in a highly abbreviated account of Saul's pursuit of David, Pseudo-Philo preserves the explicit association of prophecy and the spirit: "And (a) spirit abided in Saul, and he prophesied" (LAB 62:2).

Early rabbinic literature also attributes prophetic abilities to the Holy Spirit. In a discussion of Miriam in *Mekilta de-Rabbi Ishmael*, Tractate *Shirata* 10.58–73, for example, the question is raised concerning where in Torah Miriam is said to have been a prophetess. The biblical text quoted, Exod 2:1–3, has nothing to do with prophecy. Nevertheless, the rabbis are able to detect a veiled reference to prophecy in the vocabulary of Exod 2:4, such as the words, "afar off." How do these words point to the Holy Spirit and by association to prophecy? The rabbis argue that these words, "afar off," express the Holy Spirit's presence in Jer 31:2: "From afar the Lord appeared to me"—i.e., the Lord's presence and the Holy Spirit are related in Jeremiah 31. Based upon the exegetical principle, *gezerah shawah*, an argument from analogy drawn from two passages with a similar expression—in this case "afar off"—the rabbis can argue that the Holy Spirit, which is discernible in Jeremiah 31, is present as well in Exodus 2. The integral association of the spirit with prophecy allows the rabbis to infer then that Miriam's standing "afar off" signals her prophetic stature.

Purification and Cleansing

In many other early Jewish texts, the spirit is related to human purity and cleansing. Rabbi Nehemiah, once again in *Mekilta de-Rabbi Ishmael*, though now in Tractate *Beshallah* 7.134–36, associates obedience with reception of the spirit: "For as a reward for the faith with which Israel believed in God, the Holy Spirit rested upon them . . .

R. Nehemiah says: Whence can you prove that whosoever accepts even one single commandment with true faith is deserving of having the Holy Spirit rest upon him." In the *Testaments of the Twelve Patriarchs*, Benjamin attributes sexual purity to the spirit: "He has no pollution in his heart, because upon him is resting the spirit of God" (TBen 8.3). The *Rule of the Community* from Qumran evinces the conviction that the spirit is integrally related to purification: "by the spirit of holiness which links him with the truth he is cleansed of all his sins. And by the spirit of uprightness and of humility his sin is atoned" (1QS 3.7b-8a). In the future, the spirit will once again purify the child of light, "cleansing him with the spirit of holiness from every irreverent deed. He will sprinkle over him the spirit of truth like lustral water . . ." (1QS 4.21).

The association of purity with the spirit in the context of Community initiation is apparent as well in the Qumran hymns, where certain vocabulary can be understood to indicate drawing near to God through the Community,[1] such as in 1QH 6.13–14:

> . . . in your kindness toward humankind
> you have enlarged his share with the spirit of your holiness.
> Thus, you make me approach your intelligence,
> and to the degree that I approach
> my fervor against all those who act wickedly
> and (against) people of guile increases;
> for everyone who approaches you,
> does not defy your orders . . .

The sixteenth hymn, though fragmentary and obtuse at several points, is particularly rich with the language of approaching the Community:

> . . . to be strengthened by the spirit of holiness,
> to adhere to the truth of your covenant,
> to serve you in truth, with a perfect heart . . . (8.15)
> You have resolved, in fact, to take pity . . .
> to show me favor by the spirit of your compassion
> and by the splendor of your glory . . . (8.16–17)
> I know that no one besides you is just.
> I have appeased your face by the spirit which you have
>   given me,

> to lavish your favor on your servant for [ever,]
> to purify me with your Holy Spirit,
> to approach your will according to the extent of your
>   kindnesses (8.19–20).

Far from the shores of the Dead Sea, perhaps in Egypt, the spirit was also associated with entrance into a life of faith. In the romantic tale, *Joseph and Aseneth*, Aseneth, the daughter of Pentephres (the biblical Potiphar) is converted to Judaism by Joseph. In this story, Joseph places his hand upon Aseneth's head and prays,

> . . . and renew her by your spirit,
> and form her anew by your hidden hand,
> and make her alive again by your life,
> and let her eat your bread of life,
> and drink your cup of blessing,
> and number her among your people . . . (8:9).

Subsequently, Aseneth is led by a heavenly man to a room with a marvelous honeycomb. He says to her, "Happy are you, Aseneth, because the ineffable mysteries of the Most High have been revealed to you, and happy [are] all who attach themselves to the Lord God in repentance, because they will eat from this comb. For this comb is [full of the] spirit of life" (16:14). Finally, at a climactic moment, "Joseph put his arms around her, and Aseneth [put hers] around Joseph, and they kissed each other for a long time and both came to life in their spirit. And Joseph kissed Aseneth and gave her spirit of life, and he kissed her the second time and gave her spirit of wisdom, and he kissed her the third time and gave her spirit of truth" (19:10–11). In this lovely romance, then, as in the poetry of the Qumran sectarians, the spirit purifies and draws people into the sphere of the faithful.

This process of purification takes on a communal character in the *Rule of the Community* from Qumran (1QS 9.3–4): "When these exist in Israel in accordance with these rules in order to establish the spirit of holiness in truth eternal, in order to atone for the fault of the transgression and for the guilt of sin and for the approval for the earth, without the flesh of burnt offerings . . ." Similarly, in *Jub*

1:20–21, Moses echoes Psalm 51, adapting it to a communal setting, when he intercedes for Israel, "O Lord, let your mercy be lifted up upon your people, and create for them an upright spirit. . . . Create a pure heart and a Holy Spirit for them. And do not let them be ensnared by their sin henceforth and forever." God responds (1:22–25) in turn by echoing Psalm 51 and Ezek 11:19–20: "And I shall create for them a Holy Spirit, and I shall purify them so that they will not turn away from following me from that day and forever. And their souls will cleave to me and to all my commandments" (1:23).

The Messianic Savior

Another strand in this tapestry begins with our observation in chapter 3 that exegetical insight was attributed to the divine spirit—what Ben Sira calls "the spirit of understanding." A particularly focussed association of the spirit with wisdom emerges from the prediction in the Hebrew Bible of a just Davidic ruler who will bring in the wake of his reign both human and cosmic peace (Isa 11:1–9):

> The spirit of the LORD shall rest on him
> the spirit of wisdom and understanding
> the spirit of counsel and might
> the spirit of knowledge and the fear of the LORD
>   (Isa 11:2).

Although later developments of this figure in the Isaiah corpus preserve the relationship between justice, mercy, and the knowledge of God, the defining feature which predominates is justice. Wisdom is supplanted by justice in the exilic description of the so-called messianic servant in whom God delights: "I have put my spirit upon him; he will bring forth justice to the nations" (Isa 42:1b-c). This servant will not grow weary "until he has established justice in the earth" (Isa 42:1d). The elusive yet related prophetic figure of Isa 61:1–7, whose character was concretized during the exilic or post-exilic period, also holds justice rather than wisdom to be the fundamental project of his calling:

> The spirit of the Lord GOD is upon me
> because the LORD has anointed me
> he has sent me to bring good news to the oppressed
>   (Isa 61:1).

Despite the increasing ascendancy of justice at the expense of wisdom in the Isaiah corpus, early Jewish appropriations of these texts preserve the original association of the spirit with wisdom. The spirit which dwells upon the Elect One, the central eschatological character of the *Similitudes of Enoch*, is depicted principally, in language reminiscent of Isaiah 11, as a spirit of wisdom: "The Elect One stands before the Lord of the Spirits; his glory is forever and ever and his power is unto all generations. In him dwells the spirit of wisdom, the spirit which gives thoughtfulness, the spirit of knowledge and strength, and the spirit of those who have fallen asleep in righteousness" (*1 Enoch* 49:2–3).

Poetic depictions of the anticipated messianic deliverer, redolent of the images of Isaiah 11, emerge as well in the literature of Judaism in late antiquity. The author of the *Psalms of Solomon* preserves the association of the spirit and wisdom:

> And he will not weaken in his days, (relying) upon his God
> for God made him powerful in the Holy Spirit
> and wise in the counsel of understanding
> with strength and righteousness (17:37).

So too does the author of the *Testament of Levi*:

> And the glory of the Most High shall burst forth upon him.
> And the spirit of understanding and sanctification
> shall rest upon him . . .
> And he shall open the gates of paradise;
> he shall remove the sword that has threatened since Adam,
> and he will grant to the saints to eat of the tree of life.
> The spirit of holiness shall be upon them.
> And Beliar shall be bound by him.
> And he shall grant to his children the authority to trample
> on wicked spirits (18:7, 10–12).

In the *Melchizedek Scroll* from among the Dead Sea Scrolls (11QMelch), the figure of Isaiah 61 is transformed into a warrior figure who will destroy Belial (Beliar) and his entourage of evil spirits. These texts project an emphasis upon strength or power, which, though consistent with their own eschatological expectations of deliverance, cannot be said to arise genetically from Isaiah 11, 42, or 61.

Many other fascinating references to the divine spirit and its effects could be culled from early Jewish literature. The spirit inspires, for example, praise (LAB 32:14), military heroism (LAB 27:9–10; 36:2), the ascent of the philosophical mind (Philo, *Plant.* 18–26; *Gig.* 19–55), even rhetorical prowess and concomitant qualities of the ideal Greco-Roman ruler (Philo, *Virt.* 217–19). Those I have chosen ought to suffice to illustrate that many Jewish authors and communities grasped the enormous worth of inspiration by the spirit. Whether the product of inspiration was ecstasy or inspired interpretation, whether the mode of inspiration was leaping and indwelling, conquering, unlocking mysteries, guiding, echoing, teaching, illuminating, whether the spirit was perceived, like the demons at Delphi as an invading angel, like the spirit of understanding that rejects omens and augurs, like Socrates' demon as a customary friend, like a draught to be drunk—the literary texts we have so briefly perused suggest unequivocally that many Jewish authors in the course of half a millennium were most certainly not of two minds about experiences of which the spirit was the catalyst.

NOTES

Chapter 1

1   See especially A. Méasson, *Du char ailé de Zeus à l'Arche d'Alliance: images et mythes platoniciens chez Philon d'Alexandrie* (Paris: Études Augustiniennes, 1986); D. T. Runia, *Philo of Alexandria and the* Timaeus *of Plato* (Leiden: Brill, 1986). Philo's knowledge of Roman education is evident in his treatise, *De congressu quaerendae eruditionis gratia*, which describes the common course of education, the Encyclia, in which were included the study of literature, rhetoric, mathematics, music, and logic.

2   For an introduction to Philo and his writings, see Y. Amir, "Authority and Interpretation of Scripture in the Writings of Philo," in *Mikra: Text, Translation, Reading and Interpretation of the Hebrew Bible in Ancient Judaism and Early Christianity*, J. Mulder and H. Sysling, eds. (Assen and Philadelphia: van Gorcum and Fortress, 1988) pp. 421–53.

3   For introductions to Josephus and his writings, see H. W. Attridge, "Josephus and His Works," in *Jewish Writings of the Second Temple Period*, M. E. Stone, ed. (Assen and Philadelphia: Van Gorcum and Fortress, 1984) 185–232; and L. H. Feldman, "Use, Authority and Exegesis of Mikra in the Writings of Josephus," in *Mikra*, Mulder and Sysling, eds., pp. 455–518.

4   H. Jacobson, *A Commentary on Pseudo-Philo's* Liber Antiquitatum Biblicarum (Leiden: Brill, 1996) 1.213.

5   See "The lament of Jephthah's daughter: themes, traditions, originality," *Studi Medievali* 12.2 (1971) 825–41, 846–47.

6   For an introduction, see Jacobson, *A Commentary on Pseudo-Philo's Liber Antiquitatum Biblicarum*, 1.195–280.

7   For an introduction, see A. Di Lella, *The Wisdom of Ben Sira: A New Translation with Notes* (Garden City: Doubleday, 1987); and J. L. Crenshaw, "The Book of Ecclesiasticus," in *The New Interpreter's Bible*, L. E. Keck et al., eds. (Nashville: Abingdon, 1997) 267–360.

8   For introductions to the Dead Sea Scrolls, see J. C. VanderKam, *The Dead Sea Scrolls Today* (Grand Rapids: Eerdmans, 1994); and G. Vermes, *The Complete Dead Sea Scrolls in English* (London: Penguin, 1997 [5th ed.]).

9   For an introduction, see M. E. Stone, *Fourth Ezra* (Minneapolis: Fortress, 1990).

10   See M. Hengel, *Judaism and Hellenism: Studies in their Encounter in Palestine during the Early Hellenistic Period* (Minneapolis: Fortress, 1981). Significant critiques notwithstanding (see particularly the many important observations in L. H. Feldman, *Jew and Gentile in the Ancient World: Attitudes and Interactions From Alexander to Justinian* [Princeton: Princeton University, 1993] 3–44), Hengel has demonstrated that Greco-Roman influence may have permeated even the recesses of first-century Judaism.

Chapter 2

1   On the possibility of ecstasy in Israelite prophetic experience, see the studies of J. Lindblom, *Prophecy in Ancient Israel* (Philadelphia: Fortress, 1962) 65–82; 122–37; 173–82; and R. R. Wilson, *Prophecy and Society in Ancient Israel* (Philadelphia: Fortress, 1980), esp. pp. 32–51

2   See also Josh 24:9–10, in the context of Joshua's summary of Israelite history: "Then King Balak son of Zippor of Moab, set out to fight against Israel. He sent and invited Balaam son of Beor to curse you, but I would not listen to Balaam; therefore he blessed you; so I rescued you out of his hand." For a brief survey of the various levels of culpability attributed to Balaam by early Jewish authors, see G. Vermes, *Scripture and Tradition in Judaism* (Leiden: Brill, 1973 [2nd ed.]) 173–75. Some of the more important secondary discussions of early Jewish interpretations of Balaam in general include: G. Vermes, *Scripture and Tradition*, pp. 127–77; J. R. Baskin, *Pharaoh's Counsellors: Job, Jethro, and Balaam in Rabbinic and Patristic Tradition* (Chico, CA: Scholars, 1983) 75–113; L. H. Feldman, "Josephus' Portrait of Balaam," *Studia Philonica Annual* 5 (1993) 48–83; J. T. Greene, *Balaam and His Interpreters: A Hermeneutical History of the Balaam Traditions* (Atlanta: Scholars, 1992).

3   Num 24:2 reads, "Balaam looked up and saw Israel camping tribe by tribe. Then the spirit of God came upon him. . ." LXX Num 23:7 reads, "And the spirit of God came upon him . . ."

4   This identification was recognized by A. Schlatter, "Wie Sprach Josephus von Gott?" *Beiträge zur Förderung christlicher Theologie* 14.1 (1910) 32.

5   See also Plato *Meno* 99C; *Apology* 22C; and *Timaeus* 71E.

6   This is not to say that such features are Greco-Roman rather than Jewish. In *The Spirit in First Century Judaism* (Leiden: Brill, 1997) 109–14, I have contended that many of these features occur as well in the literature of Early Judaism.

7   See also Plato, *Timaeus* 71E; Cicero, *Div.* 1.129.

8   M. E. Stone (*Fourth Ezra*, p. 120) contends correctly that this statement about the retention of memory constitutes a "deliberate" reversal of this *topos*, i.e., the loss of memory.

9   Translation from Post-Nicene Fathers, 1.289.

10   Translation from Ante-Nicene Fathers, 11.366.

11   Or Firmianus. He probably lived ca. 240–320 CE.

Chapter 3

1   Cicero, *Div.* 1.66–67.

2   Lucan, *De bello civili* 5.169–77.

3   *Sibylline Oracles* 3.3, 7.

4   This is the title of an important chapter in E. R. Dodds' *The Greeks and the Irrational* (Berkeley: University of California, 1951).

5   For details, see my *Spirit*, pp. 178–83.

6   The author of Zech 7:12 refers to the "former prophets" when he explains in his retrospective analysis of Israelite history the cause of the exile: "They made their hearts adamant in order not to hear the law and the words that the LORD of hosts had sent by his spirit through the former prophets. Therefore great wrath came from the LORD of hosts."

7   Translation mine.

8   See also 1QH 13.19; 16.11; 17.17.

9   Josephus' description of the Essenes, though it too offers little insight into the particular mode of inspiration, associates an uncanny ability to predict the future with knowledge of the sacred texts of Israel: "There are some among them [the Essenes] who profess to foretell the future, being versed from their early years in holy books, various forms of purification and apophthegms of prophets; and seldom, if ever, do they err in their predictions." The emphasis upon reliability, coupled with the positive descriptions elsewhere of Essenes who reliably predicted the future (Judas in *Bell.* 1.78; Simon in *Bell.* 2.113; and Menahem in *Ant.* 13.311), suggests that Josephus' belief in the ability to predict rests at least in part upon a need for knowledge of the holy books.

10   E.g., *Leg. All.* 3.228; *Conf. Ling.* 159; *Cher.* 69; *Som.* 1.23; *Spec. Leg.* 1.63; 4.50; *Her.* 98; *Vit. Mos.* 1.68.

11   Translation mine.

12   See M. Pohlenz, "Philon von Alexandria," *Nachrichten von der Akademie der Wissenschaften in Göttingen, Philologisch-historische Klasse* 5 (1942) 473.

Chapter 4

1   H. W. Kuhn, *Enderwartung und gegenwärtiges Heil: Untersuchungen zu den Gemeindeliedern von Qumran* (Göttingen: Vandenhoeck & Ruprecht, 1966) 117–39. Kuhn discerns initiation language as well in 1QH 12.11–12; 13.19; 14.13, and f 3.14.

About the Author

John R. Levison earned a B.A. from Wheaton College, an M.A. from Cambridge University and a Ph.D. from Duke University. He is currently associate professor of the practice of biblical interpretation at The Divinity School of Duke University. In addition to dozens of articles, he has published five other books: *The Spirit in First Century Judaism* (Brill, 1999), *Josephus' Contra Apionem: Studies in Its Character and Context with a Latin Concordance to the Portion Missing in Greek* (editor, with Louis Feldman; Brill, 1996), *Jesus in Global Contexts* (with Priscilla Pope-Levison; Westminster/ John Knox, 1992), *Portraits of Adam in Early Judaism* (JSP Supplement Series 1, and *Return to Babel: Global Perspectives on the Bible* (editor, with Priscilla Pope-Levison, Westminster/John Knox, 1999). He has been the co-chair of the Divine Mediator Figures in Antiquity Group of the Society of Biblical Literature, a contributing reviewer for *Old Testament Abstracts*, and currently serves on the editorial board of the *Journal for the Study of the Pseudepigrapha*.